Skills for Effective Learning in

One of the five books in the *Mental Health and Wellbeing Teacher Toolkit*, this practical resource focuses on the topic of 'Skills for Learning'. The book offers research-driven, practical strategies, resources and lesson plans to support educators and health professionals. This is a resource book for practitioners looking to have a positive impact on the mental health and wellbeing of the children and young people in their care; both now and in the future.

Chapters span key topics including Metacognition, Learning Dimensions, Problem Solving and Cognitive Strategies. A complete toolkit for teachers and counsellors, this book offers:

◆ Easy to follow and flexible lesson plans that can be adapted and personalised for use in lessons or smaller groups or 1:1 work

◆ Resources that are linked to the PSHE and Wellbeing curriculum for KS1, KS2 and KS3

◆ New research, 'Circles for Learning', where the introduction of baby observation into the classroom by a teacher is used to understand and develop self-awareness, skills for learning, relationships, neuroscience and awareness of others

◆ Sections on the development of key skills in communication, skills for learning, collaboration, empathy and self-confidence

◆ Learning links, learning objectives and reflection questions.

Offering research-driven, practical strategies and lesson plans, *Skills for Effective Learning in School* is an essential resource book for educators and health professionals looking to have a positive impact on the mental health and wellbeing of the children in their care; both now and in the future.

Alison Waterhouse has worked in mainstream, special education and the independent sector for the past 30 years, specialising in working with children with AEN including Mental Health and Wellbeing. She has set up and developed an Independent Therapeutic Special School; developed a role as Teacher in Charge of the Social and Emotional Wellbeing of the Whole School Community, and has been an Inclusion Manager and Deputy Head in mainstream schools. She now works as an Independent Educational Consultant for SEN and Wellbeing, is involved in staff training; and has her own Educational Psychotherapy practice. Alison works with children who are referred due to difficulties with self-esteem, anger, anxiety, depression and other Mental Health needs as well as children with learning differences. Alison is developing the Circles for Learning Project in schools and has already undertaken a Primary Research Project and is now working on a Secondary Research Project. The resources were put together to support staff with these projects.

Skills for effective learning in school

Positive relationships in school

The brain and learning

Self-discovery

Emotional literacy

The invisible roots of learning

Skills for Effective Learning in School

Supporting Emotional Health and Wellbeing

Alison Waterhouse

Routledge
Taylor & Francis Group

LONDON AND NEW YORK

First published 2019
by Routledge
2 Park Square, Milton Park, Abingdon, Oxon OX14 4RN

and by Routledge
52 Vanderbilt Avenue, New York, NY 10017

Routledge is an imprint of the Taylor & Francis Group, an informa business

British Library Cataloguing-in-Publication Data
A catalogue record for this book is available from the British Library

Library of Congress Cataloging-in-Publication Data
A catalog record for this book has been requested

ISBN: 978-1-138-37031-9 (pbk)
ISBN: 978-0-429-42806-7 (ebk)

Typeset in Avant Garde
by Apex CoVantage, LLC

To Melanie, one of the best teachers I have ever had the privilege of working with. Thank you for all your support, advice and for believing in the power of Circles for Learning.

Contents

Contents

Introduction

SKILLS FOR EFFECTIVE LEARNING

Learning is a hugely broad concept which includes not only the acquisition of knowledge but the evolution of skills, understanding, strategies, experience and how we think about these. There has been a vast amount of scientific research published over the past 20 years linked to learning and the process of learning. Many theories of learning, education and practice have been put forward and developed by a range of very prominent people.

Many argue that Johann Pestalozzi should be thought of as the starting point of modern education theory and practice. He argued that security in the home was the foundation of happiness and learning (Peltzman 1998). Froebel was the first person to articulate a full theory on how children learn and this led to the idea of education having a philosophy (Sniegoski 1994). Maria Montessori based her philosophy on observations stating that education or learning begins at birth (Montessori 2004). Susan Isaacs also promoted the importance of observation in working with children. Her interest in psychoanalysis led her to examine the importance of a child's emotional development and not just their acquisition of knowledge or skills (Pound 2005). Piaget's theories dominated in the 1960s and 70s and were promoted within teacher training (Beard 1969). Vygotsky again promoted the importance of observation in teaching and learning and also argued the importance of planning the curriculum to challenge a child's current ability (Pound 2005). Like Piaget, he argued that knowledge and understanding are constructed by the child dependent upon their experiences.

Skinner created his behaviourism learning theory where he argued that all behaviour is learnt and that it can be shaped by punishment and rewards (Fosnot 1996). His work became widely applied to child development. Many argue that this way of working ignores the emotional states and complex motives that make up human behaviour.

Albert Bandura developed his Social Learning Theory which he later developed into his Cognitive Learning Theory (Fosnot 1996). Unlike the behaviourists, who believed that learning occurs through reinforcement and punishment, Bandura suggested that learning occurs through the observation of others and within a social setting. He also argued that this learning is subject to the internal mental states of the learner. His theory highlighted the importance of social influence and the importance of reinforcement in both acquiring and changing behaviours.

Learning is the process of moving from a state of not knowing to a state of knowing for a benefit, thus enabling the learner to achieve something that they were not able to do before. Central to this belief is the idea that the learner wishes to learn or acquire a new skill or piece of knowledge which means that they must be aware of themselves as a learner. Learning now becomes the vehicle to achieving something and is thus personal however it also becomes an end product of that process.

Introduction

The word education is related to the Greek word *educere* – to bring out or develop potential; it is therefore involved with the respectful cultivation of learning. Guy Claxton argues that education for the 21st century must enable young people to manage complex issues that they will face with skill and confidence (Claxton et al. 2011). He divides the focus of education into two distinct areas: content curriculum and learning curriculum. The content curriculum he describes as valuable and exciting areas of study and the learning curriculum he argues is the attitudes, values and habits towards learning. These attributes have been given a variety of labels over the years including Skills for Learning.

Three areas are needed to ensure learning is both successful and positive:

1. A range of tools, skills, beliefs and attitudes which are linked to the learner themselves, making them an effective learner.

2. An effective learning environment – an environment that supports the learning process in a positive way.

3. The teacher/facilitator. This can be a person who can model the skills needed, or a person who has the skills and abilities to coach the learner, peers to observe, a learning partner to collaborate with, or a teacher to explain, orchestrate, and commentate, all of which have an impact on the learning journey of children and young people (CYP).

Claxton argues that 21st-century education should be aiming to support CYP in developing a capacity to learn. This learning capacity is vital in supporting CYP to meet the general challenges of life in this century (Claxton 2004).

Claxton defines learning dispositions as the capacities needed for the power to learn, or Learning Power. Learning Power is the way you think about your mind and how you feel about yourself rather than the intelligence you were born with.

Ruth Deakin Crick suggests that Learning Power is at the heart of the ecology of the classroom and that the role of the teacher is to create the optimal ecology for the children to grow, learn and thrive. The research evidence from the Effective Lifelong Learning Inventory (ELLI) project identified 7 dimensions of Learning Power, all of which support learning. Each dimension has an opposite, with an emerging pole being positive for learning and a contrast pole which tends to inhibit learning (Crick et al. 2004).

1. Changing and learning ←——————→ Being static or stuck

2. Curiosity ←——————→ Passivity

3. Meaning making ←——————→ Fragmentation

4. Creativity ←——————→ Rule-boundedness

5. Learning relationships ←——————→ Isolation or dependence

6. Strategic awareness ←——————→ Behaving like a robot

7. Resilience ←——————→ Dependence and fragility

There is a strong body of evidence from Psychology and Education that shows the importance of metacognition and self-regulation to effective student learning. Self-regulation is about the extent that learners are aware of their own strengths and weaknesses and the strategies that they use to learn. Self-regulation describes how a young person motivates themselves to engage with the learning task and how they use the strategies to support themselves and how their learning improves over time.

It can be divided into 3 main areas:

Cognition – the mental process involved in knowing, understanding and learning. This includes cognitive strategies like memorisation or subject specific strategies like the use of different brush strokes in art.

Metacognition – the way the learner monitors and shapes the learning task, i.e. having chosen a cognitive strategy such as memorisation, they monitor how that strategy is working, if it is managing the task and how well it is working.

Motivation – the willingness to engage both cognition and metacognition and use them to learn.

Cognition, metacognition and motivation all interact in a complex way during learning.

THE CIRCLES FOR LEARNING PROJECT

Circles for Learning is a unique research-based, whole class or small group project that builds the positive foundations for Mental Health and Wellbeing. It supports and strengthens learning skills alongside the development of social skills, emotional literacy and wellbeing. It facilitates and encourages children to experience how learning happens and explore brain development, relationships and emotions. This includes how other people might feel or experience situations, how to manage emotions, discover our sense of self and understand how our beliefs influence our behaviour.

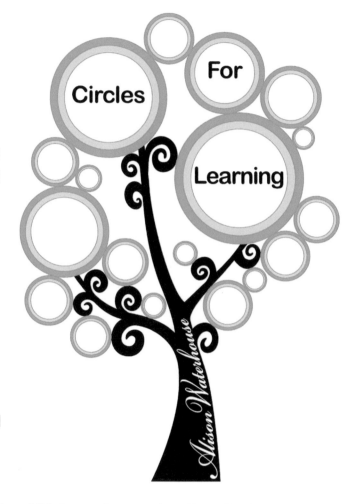

Circles for Learning has been developed by Alison Waterhouse over the past five years. Alison initiated the Circles for Learning Project in primary schools in East Sussex, where she led and developed this innovative way of working with children. As colleagues became aware of her work, they asked to get involved, so Alison set up the Primary Research Project for five schools in East Sussex where she worked closely with the class teachers to both design and develop the project in their schools. This enabled her to work in both small

rural schools and very deprived large urban schools as well as with a variety of teachers. As a result of the interest of professionals in the Secondary field, Alison has just completed a research project with 4 different secondary schools to explore and measure the impact of the work within their environment. This work has been the core of a research MA in Education with the University of York.

The project trains and then supports teachers to bring a parent and baby into the classroom once a month for a year. The children and young people are supported in observing the interactions, learning, relationships and the baby's early developing sense of self. Then, with the support of the teacher, they explore and think about what they have seen and how this may link to their own development, thinking, behaviour and ways of interacting with others.

These observations are the provocation or stimulus to follow-up work led by the teacher exploring one of the Circles for Learning's five areas of work:

1. Emotional competencies: including recognising emotions, managing our own emotions, recognising emotions in others and developing strategies to cope and deal with these emotions.

2. Relationships: including social skills, the learning relationship, social inclusion and empathy.

3. Self-discovery: including self-concept, self-esteem, self-efficacy, self-regulation, self-talk, self-compassion, mindsets and resilience.

4. Skills for effective learning.

5. Neuroscience and learning.

These five key areas form the foundations for Mental Health and Wellbeing. The follow-up work is not a scheme of work to be followed regardless of the needs of the children or young people but a wide range of activities that the teacher can refer to and use that supports the needs of the group at that time.

The resources within each of the five books in the *Mental Health and Wellbeing Toolkit* can be used as standalone resources to support the five key areas that create the foundations for Mental Health and Wellbeing or as part of the Circles for Learning Project.

TRACKING SHEET

NAME/GROUP:		
DATE:		**TERM:**
ASSESSMENTS UNDERTAKEN:		**OTHER INFORMATION:**
Date	Lesson:	Comments
Date	Lesson:	Comments
Date	Lesson:	Comments
Date	Lesson:	Comments
Date	Lesson:	Comments
Date	Lesson:	Comments
Date	Lesson:	Comments
Date	Lesson:	Comments
Date	Lesson:	Comments
Date	Lesson:	Comments

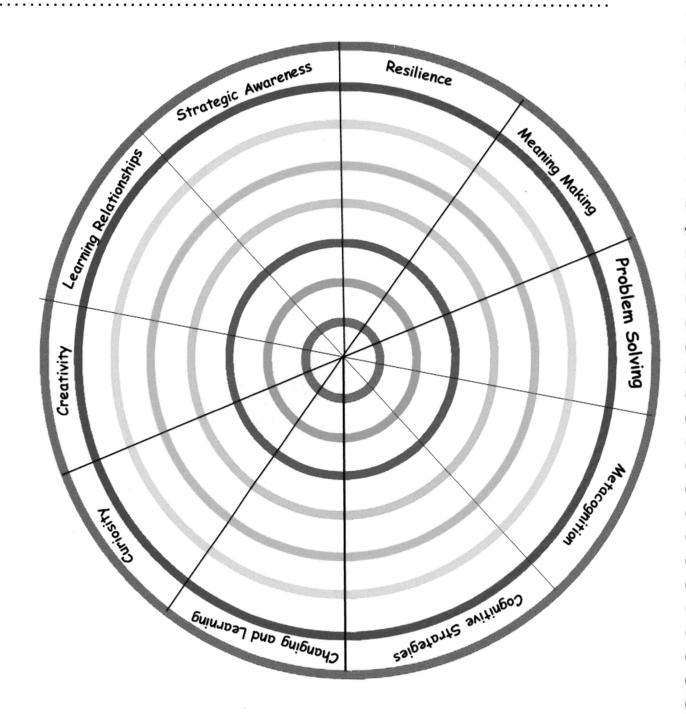

The circular tracking document has been designed to allow practitioners to monitor and track the areas that they have covered with the children. As each lesson is covered they are entered onto the document within the focus section. This enables practitioners to see the particular focus they are taking with their group. For some classes they may present a high need within a particular area or a strength in another area and so this can be shown and monitored. The document also allows for other lessons/activities to be added to the document that may have extended knowledge and understanding in this area from PSHE or Circle Time focus.

The document allows the flexibility to meet the needs of the children as they arise rather than having to follow a pre-set curriculum and in so doing allows practitioners to clearly see the areas of need and what they are doing to meet them.

Chapter 1

Metacognition

Thinking about thinking!

SESSION OBJECTIVES

To develop an understanding about what a thought is and how thinking about our thinking supports us with our learning.

SESSION OUTCOMES

✓ To be able to share our ideas about thinking.

✓ To be able to verbalise our thinking about learning.

✓ To be able to define metacognition.

LESSON PLAN

➢ Remind the children about a time when they watched their class baby 'think' about a task.

➢ Support the children to remember and think about a time when they watched their baby undertaking a task and their parent watching and thinking about them.

For those classrooms not able to undertake the Circles for Learning Project, video clips or photographs can be used to support the discussion around the topic and stimulate thoughts and ideas from the children and young people.

Task

KS1: To explore where they think best and what they need to be able to think well.

KS2: To create something using a selection of 'junk' and share their thinking process.

KS3: To explore ways that they learn facts for a test and then create their own revision resource.

Metacognition

KS1

1. Read the book *I am Henry Finch* by Alexis Deacon and Vivian Schwartz.

2. Ask the children about how Henry felt about thinking and what he needed to be able to think.

3. Explore where they think best and what they need to think.

4. Ask the children to draw a thought that they had about the book.

KS2

1. Read the book *Going Places* by Peter and Paul Reynolds.

2. Discuss what they thought about the book.

3. Ask the children to work individually or in small groups. Give each group the same variety of 'junk' and ask them to make something as a group.

4. As they work, ask them to draw the different thoughts that they had inside the thought bubbles to create a thinking timeline.

5. Create a small exhibition showing the creation and their thinking timeline.

6. Discuss their thinking as a group after the exhibition. What did they learn about their thinking process?

KS3

1. Share a short historical information sheet with the young people.

2. Ask them to create a resource to help them learn the information for a test.

3. Discuss their immediate thoughts – even if they are negative? Share them as a group.

4. Ask the young people to work in small groups, pairs or on their own and document their thinking process using the metacognition question sheet.

5. Ask the young people to create their resource.

6. Share the resources and the metacognition question sheet as a walk around exhibition.

7. Discuss what they have learnt from undertaking the task and from looking at what other people have done.

RESOURCES

1. *I am Henry Finch* by Alexis Deacon and Vivian Schwartz

2. Thought bubbles

3. *Going Places* by Peter and Paul Reynolds

4. Thought bubble timeline

5. Metacognition question diagram

IMPORTANT POINTS

We are often not aware of our thinking. However, if we stop and think about our thinking it can help us to learn and review our learning.

LEARNING LINKS

Metacognition, planning and reviewing work.

REFLECTION

Questions:

Positive comment from child:

Positive comment from adult:

LEARNING DIMENSIONS		SOCIAL & EMOTIONAL SKILLS	
Strategic awareness	▓	Emotional literacy	
Learning relationships		Neuroscience	
Curiosity		Self-regulation	
Creativity	▓	Self-development	▓
Meaning making	▓		
Changing & learning	▓		
Resilience			

METACOGNITION QUESTION DIAGRAM

Planning our project

SESSION OBJECTIVES

To explore and develop a greater understanding for the importance of planning in learning.

SESSION OUTCOMES

✓ To be able to plan a project and then complete the task.

✓ To be able to share and discuss how you went about the task and why.

LESSON PLAN

➢ Ask the children to remember a time when they watched their class baby work out how to do something.

➢ Identify the different strategies that they used.

For those classrooms not able to undertake the Circles for Learning Project, video clips or photographs can be used to support the discussion around the topic and stimulate thoughts and ideas from the children and young people.

Task

KS1: To plan and then make a mask.
KS2: To create a game to enable a friend to learn something.
KS3: To create a game to enable a friend to learn something for a test/exam.

KS1

1. Lay out a range of resources on a table.

2. Set the task – your challenge is to make a mask for your friend.

3. Ask the children to walk around and look at the resource but not take anything.

4. Ask the children to go and think about what they want to do.

5. Give the children 6 sticky notes and ask them to write on the sticky notes steps that they need to do to achieve the task. And then stick them in the correct order on the desk.

6. Alternatively give the children a list of actions and ask them to put them in order so that they can complete the task.

7. Ask the children to follow their plan and make a mask.

8. Ask them to note any time when they changed their plan.

9. Discuss what they did and why and ask the children to reflect on their plan – did it work? Would they change anything next time? Did they alter it in any way, if so why?

10. Share different ways to make a plan – flow diagram and planning sheets.

KS2/KS3

1. Share a range of planning ideas with the children – flow diagrams, planning sheets and a Gantt chart.

2. Discuss the different ways people like to plan.

3. Ask them to share how they plan a task?

4. Set the challenge – they need to create and then make a game to help a friend learn something – this could be a game to help learn spellings of a times table or specific facts in a subject.

5. Ask them to plan their task: work out which friend they are going to support, decide what they are going to help them with and write a list of things they need. They can do this in any way they wish.

6. Ask the children and young people to share their planning and talk about how they devised it and why.

7. Follow planning to make the game.

RESOURCES

1. Planning sheet – example

2. Flow diagram sheet – example

3. Sticky notes

4. Actions slips

IMPORTANT POINTS

That planning organises our thoughts and allows us to 'see' how we will undertake a project.

LEARNING LINKS

Metacognition, learning skills.

REFLECTION

Questions:

Positive comment from child:

Positive comment from adult:

LEARNING DIMENSIONS		SOCIAL & EMOTIONAL SKILLS	
Strategic awareness	░	Emotional literacy	
Learning relationships	░	Neuroscience	
Curiosity		Self-regulation	
Creativity	░	Self-development	░
Meaning making			
Changing & learning	░		
Resilience			

FLOW DIAGRAM

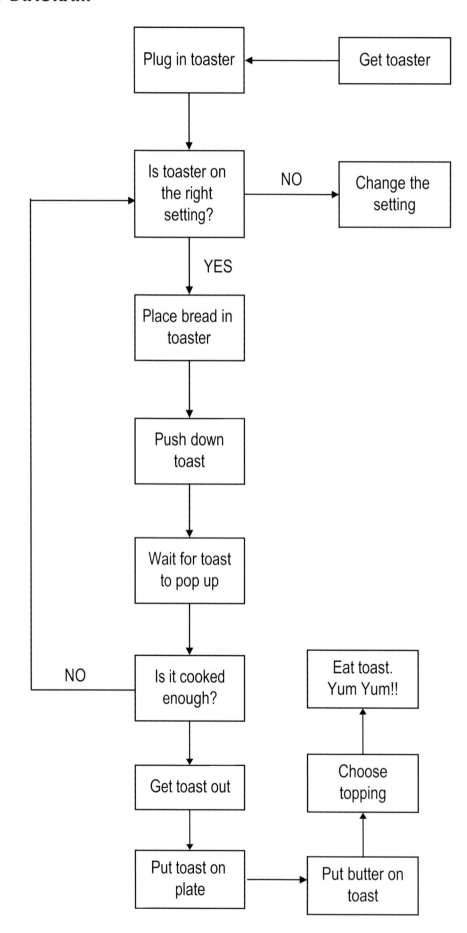

Notice Board Planning Sheet

Theme of board:

Dates of display:

Titles or words needed:

Backing paper colours:

Border design:

Student work to be displayed:

Graphics/pictures needed:

Layout of board:

MAKING A MASK FOR A FRIEND

Look at all the resources and imagine what I could use them for.	Think about what sort of mask to make. What would my friend like?
Decide which friend to make a mask for.	Draw a rough sketch of what I would like the mask to look like.
Draw or write the parts of the face and then decide what to use for each one.	Go and get all the resources I need.
Decide what to use to make the mask on.	Find the base of my mask.
Lay out the parts of my mask and look and see if I like it. If I don't like it, change it until I do.	Stick all the pieces on my mask.
Show the mask to my friend.	

Monitoring our learning

SESSION OBJECTIVES

To understand the importance of monitoring our learning and having the courage to change things if needed.

SESSION OUTCOMES

✓ To be able to verbalise the learning journey of a task.

✓ To be able to explain why they did what they did and, if they changed direction, why.

LESSON PLAN

➢ Ask the children to remember a time when they watched their class baby when they were trying to achieve something.

➢ Discuss the different strategies they used to get what they wanted.

For those classrooms not able to undertake the Circles for Learning Project, video clips or photographs can be used to support the discussion around the topic and stimulate thoughts and ideas from the children and young people.

Task

KS1: To be able to describe how they made a box/bag for their mask.
KS2: To be able to talk about how they made a box/bag for their learning game for a friend.
KS3: To be able to talk about how they made an advert for their learning game for a friend.

KS1/KS2

1. Ask the children to think about how they planned and then made their masks. Did their planning work or did they have to adapt things?

2. Discuss what it felt like when things didn't quite work.

3. Discuss what it was like to change things as they went – how did it make them feel?

4. Set the challenge for making a box or bag to put their mask in for their friend.

5. Show them what you have available to use.

6. Share some of the things you already have that would work as boxes or bags to put the mask in. Explore how these might help you.

7. Ask the children to make their boxes or bags and tell them that you will be stopping them as they work to record how they are doing.

8. Stop at periodic points and ask the children:

   a) How the work is going – out of 10, 10 being really well, 1 being very badly. (You could draw this as a graph to show the ups and downs of a project.)

   b) How they are feeling

   c) Whether it has gone as they planned – yes or no

   d) What adaptions have they made?

   e) How did it feel when things went badly? What was their emotion? What strategies did they use to help themselves get it right and keep going?

   f) Share together the information that you have collected at the end.

9. Read *The Most Magnificent Thing* by Ashley Spires and talk about how the little girl felt and what strategies she used.

10. Create a class poster to remind the children of the importance of monitoring what they are doing in their learning and that sometimes they have to be brave and change things.

KS3

1. Ask the young people to share the experience they had of making a Learning Game for their friend. How many had had to change their plan?

2. How did this feel at the time? What strategies did they use to support themselves change things?

3. Ask the young people to make an advert for their learning game for a friend. Explain that you will stop them at intervals to ask some questions about how things are going.

4. Divide the session up into Research Time, Thinking Time, Making Time and Sharing Time.

5. Get the young people to rate each section as to which was the most difficult.

6. Discuss as a group how things went.

7. Ask the children for one thing they have learnt form the session that they will take away and use.

RESOURCES

1. Cardboard, sticky tape, glue, scissors, staples, paper, rulers, rubbers

2. Large sheets of paper

3. Felt tip pens

4. A selection of boxes

IMPORTANT POINTS

If we monitor what we are doing as we go we can change direction if needed and achieve a good outcome.

LEARNING LINKS

Changing and learning, self-awareness, metacognition.

REFLECTION

Questions:

Positive comment from child:

Positive comment from adult:

LEARNING DIMENSIONS		SOCIAL & EMOTIONAL SKILLS	
Strategic awareness		Emotional literacy	
Learning relationships		Neuroscience	
Curiosity		Self-regulation	
Creativity		Self-development	
Meaning making			
Changing & learning			
Resilience			

Reviewing our work

SESSION OBJECTIVES

To be able to share a learning journey and identify what went well, not so well and what to do differently next time.

SESSION OUTCOMES

✓ To be able to share a piece of learning and describe what happened, how it felt and the end result.

✓ To be able to describe the feelings encountered whilst undergoing the task.

✓ To be able to share the positive aspect of the learning and the difficulties encountered.

✓ To be able to describe what would be done differently next time.

LESSON PLAN

➤ Ask the children to remember a time when their class baby had learnt to do something - and then describe what the baby did. (Often babies learn by repeating the actions again and again.)

➤ Help the children talk about the emotions of a learning task and then write them on the board.

➤ Support the children in being able to identify strategies they have used to keep going when the learning became difficult.

For those classrooms not able to undertake the Circles for Learning Project, video clips or photographs can be used to support the discussion around the topic and stimulate thoughts and ideas from the children and young people.

Task

KS1: To be able to describe difficulties that they had overcome when completing the task of making a mask for a friend or making a box for the mask.

KS2: To be able to describe the difficulties and the emotions they had encountered when creating a Learning Game to help a friend learn something.

KS3: To be able to discuss the learning journey they had experienced in making the Learning Game for their friend and the follow up advert.

KS1/2

1. Children to discuss a difficulty they had encountered when completing the task.

2. Discuss the strategies that were used to overcome the difficulties.

3. Complete the review sheet.

4. Share these together.

5. Ask the children to identify a strategy that they have never used before to support learning and try this out.

KS3

1. Ask the young people to complete the learning journey review sheet.

2. Share the reviews and discuss the emotions encountered whilst working and the benefits or deficits of these.

3. Discuss the difficulties encountered and the strategies used to overcome these.

4. Collect the learning that the young people gained and how they think this might help them in the future.

RESOURCES

1. Review sheet for KS1

2. Review sheet for KS2/3

IMPORTANT POINTS

Monitoring and reviewing learning is an important feature of undertaking any learning task.

LEARNING LINKS

Metacognition, monitoring.

REFLECTION

Questions:

Positive comment from child:

Positive comment from adult:

LEARNING DIMENSIONS		SOCIAL & EMOTIONAL SKILLS	
Strategic awareness		Emotional literacy	
Learning relationships		Neuroscience	
Curiosity		Self-regulation	
Creativity		Self-development	
Meaning making			
Changing & learning			
Resilience			

LEARNING REVIEW SHEET KS1

What was the task?

....

HOW MUCH DID YOU ENJOY THE TASK?

😊 ——————————————————————— 🙁

What was 1 thing you liked about the task?

....

What was 1 thing you didn't like about this task?

....

How did you feel when you started the task?

....

How did you feel in the middle of the task?

....

How did you feel at the end of the task?

....

What is one thing you have learnt?

....

LEARNING REVIEW SHEET KS2/3

What was the task?

1. **Which stage did you enjoy the most?**

   Planning, Doing, Monitoring, Reviewing

2. **What did you learn in the planning stage?**

   ....

3. **What did you learn by monitoring your learning?**

   ....

4. **What would you do differently next time?**

   ....

5. **Name 3 emotions you experienced when undertaking the task**

   ....

6. **What went well in the project?**

   ....

7. **What didn't go well in the project?**

   ....

8. **What strategies did you use to overcome your difficulties?**

   ....

9. **What is a new strategy you have observed someone else using?**

   ....

Metacognitive talking

SESSION OBJECTIVES

To enable children and young people to teach a task to another person by modelling, describing what they are doing, how they are managing and what the end result is like.

SESSION OUTCOMES

✓ To be able to teach another child or young person how to do something using metacognitive talking.

LESSON PLAN

➢ Remind the children of a time when they observed their class mum show their class baby how to do something.

➢ Discuss the 'teaching' of the task and highlight aspects that made it successful or not.

For those classrooms not able to undertake the Circles for Learning Project, video clips or photographs can be used to support the discussion around the topic and stimulate thoughts and ideas from the children and young people.

Task

KS1: To teach another child how to make a paper aeroplane.
KS2: To teach another child how to make an origami crane.
KS3: To teach another young person how to make an origami animal.

KS1/2

1. Divide the class into 2 groups.

2. Give one group the instructions on how to make a paper aeroplane/origami crane.

3. Allow them to work together to learn how to make it.

4. Ask them to talk about what they are doing and how it feels as they are learning to do this.

5. Once they have learnt how to do this, ask them to teach a partner how to make the plane/crane.

6. When they are teaching, ask the child who is learning to talk about their learning – how they feel, how they are finding the task, what they are thinking as they learn.

7. Return to the group and discuss the experience. Share the process of talking ourselves through a task as a way to support our learning.

8. KS2 – Read *Peace Crane* together.

KS3

1. Ask the young people to find a simple origami animal to make. Working in small groups ask them to share their thinking and feelings when learning to make the animal.

2. Ask each person to choose a partner and teach them how to make the origami animal. The teacher and the learner need to share their experiences by talking out loud. This includes how difficult or easy they are finding the task, the instructions themselves and their feelings about their learning.

3. Share their experiences as a group.

4. What helped them keep going when the learning got tough?

5. What strategies did their partner use to help them?

6. What strategies did they use to keep themselves motivated and achieve the task?

RESOURCES

1. Instructions on how to make a paper aeroplane

2. Instructions on how to make an origami crane

3. *Peace Crane* by Sheila Hamanaka

4. Origami paper

5. Access to computers and the internet for research or books on origami

IMPORTANT POINTS

Learning is a process and it helps to talk ourselves through this.

LEARNING LINKS

Metacognition, learning, self-awareness.

REFLECTION

Questions:

Positive comment from child:

Positive comment from adult:

LEARNING DIMENSIONS		SOCIAL & EMOTIONAL SKILLS	
Strategic awareness		Emotional literacy	
Learning relationships		Neuroscience	
Curiosity		Self-regulation	
Creativity		Self-development	
Meaning making			
Changing & learning			
Resilience			

Chapter 2

Learning dimensions

Curiosity

A wish to know, find out and dig beneath the surface

Exploring questions 1

SESSION OBJECTIVES

To investigate how questions can help us explore a theme and find out information.

SESSION OUTCOMES

✓ A list of questions about an object.

✓ A list of different question types.

• Decide which group of questions gives you the most information.

LESSON PLAN

➤ Ask the children to think of a time when their class baby had asked a question.

➤ Explore together why we ask questions – what is their purpose?

For those classrooms not able to undertake the Circles for Learning Project, video clips or photographs can be used to support the discussion around the topic and stimulate thoughts and ideas from the children and young people.

Task

KS1: To work together to create a list of questions to find out about an object.

KS2: To work together to create a list of questions to find out information about a story.

KS3: To work together to generate a list of different sorts of questions to support finding information.

KS1

1. Explain to the children that you are going to divide them up into teams.

2. Give each team an object and ask the children to come up with as many different questions as they can to gather information about the object.

3. When the teams have come up with their list of questions ask them to share them with the class.

4. Discuss the questions and how useful they might be. Choose the best questions from each team and give a reason.

5. Ask the children how they might find out the answers to the questions they have created.

6. Choose three questions that the class really want answered and then support them finding out the answers.

KS2

1. Read the story *The Three Questions* to the children.

2. Discuss what the story tells us.

3. Share an object with the class (one that they would not know or have seen) and ask them to come up with as many questions as they can in 10 minutes.

4. Explore the questions and see if groups emerge – understanding reasons, places or setting questions, time questions, questions about characters etc.

5. Ask each child to choose their favourite question and give a reason why.

6. If they could ask 3 questions to any authors, who would they ask and what would their questions be?

KS3

1. Explain to the children that you are going to divide them up into teams.

2. Give each team a picture book with no words and ask the children to come up with as many different questions as they can to gather information about the story.

3. When the teams have come up with their list of questions ask them to share their book with the class and then share their top 5 questions and explain their reasons.

4. Discuss the questions and how useful they might be at finding out information. Choose the best 3 questions from each team and give a reason.

5. If they could ask the authors/illustrators of the books 3 questions what would they be?

RESOURCES

1. Objects – one for each team

2. Sticky notes or strips of paper

3. Pens

4. *The Three Questions* by Jon J. Muth

5. *Why?* By Nikolai Popov

6. *Meh* by Deborah Malcom

7. *The Journey* by Aaron Becker

IMPORTANT POINTS

• Questions help us find out more information about something.

• Questions can be put in groups or categories.

LEARNING LINKS

Speaking and listening, collaboration, information processing, questioning, observation.

REFLECTION

Questions:

Positive comment from child:

Positive comment from adult:

Learning dimensions

LEARNING DIMENSIONS		SOCIAL & EMOTIONAL SKILLS	
Strategic awareness	▓	Emotional literacy	▓
Learning relationships		Neuroscience	
Curiosity	▓	Self-regulation	
Creativity		Self-development	▓
Meaning making	▓		
Changing & learning	▓		
Resilience			

Exploring questions 2

SESSION OBJECTIVES

To investigate how questions can help us explore a theme and find out information.

SESSION OUTCOMES

✓ To create a Question Table Top Reminder.

LESSON PLAN

➢ Ask the children to remember a time when their class baby started asking questions.

➢ Discuss how their class parent answered them.

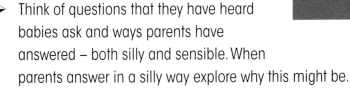

➢ Think of questions that they have heard babies ask and ways parents have answered – both silly and sensible. When parents answer in a silly way explore why this might be.

For those classrooms not able to undertake the Circles for Learning Project, video clips or photographs can be used to support the discussion around the topic and stimulate thoughts and ideas from the children and young people.

Task

KS2/3

1. Pair up the children and ask them to write a word on a piece of paper.

2. Swap over the pieces of paper and ask them to write the question with the word as the answer.

3. Share the words and the questions in the class.

4. Discuss how questions can help us be curious and find out things. Ask the question 'Is being curious a good thing?' Each pair needs to come up with a statement saying if they believe curiosity is good/bad and a reason for this.

5. Are there any famous sayings about curiosity? Collect as many as possible.

6. Share the Question Quadrant with the children and young people.

7. Read *The Island* by Armin Greder.

8. Create a quadrant for this book and explore the questions that arise.

9. Design and make a Question Table Top Reminder stating what a question is and why questions are good and the different types/groups of questions that can be used.

10. What do they think the greatest questions of all time might be?

11. As a class come up with a class list of questions.

12. Share the greatest 101 questions:

https://www.telegraph.co.uk/news/newstopics/howaboutthat/4696372/Greatest-101-questions-of-all-time-1-20.html (accessed 1 January 2019).

RESOURCES

1. *The Island* by Armin Greder

2. The Question Quadrant

3. Card

4. Pens

IMPORTANT POINTS

• Questions help us find out more information about something.

• Questions can be put in groups or categories.

LEARNING LINKS

Speaking and listening, collaboration, information processing, questioning, observation.

REFLECTION

Questions:

Positive comment from child:

Positive comment from adult:

LEARNING DIMENSIONS		SOCIAL & EMOTIONAL SKILLS	
Strategic awareness	▓	Emotional literacy	▓
Learning relationships		Neuroscience	
Curiosity	▓	Self-regulation	
Creativity		Self-development	▓
Meaning making			
Changing & learning	▓		
Resilience			

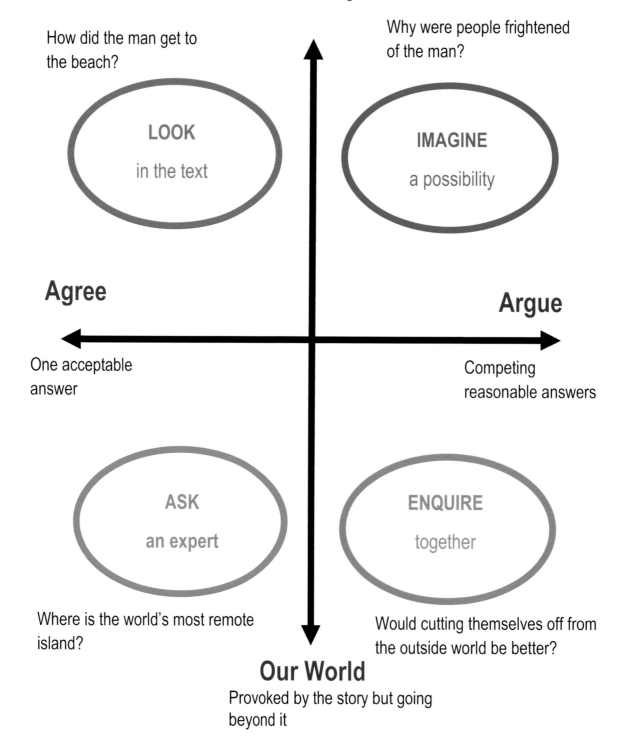

About the characters or story

Stimulus/Story World

How did the man get to
the beach?

LOOK

in the text

Why were people frightened
of the man?

IMAGINE

a possibility

Agree

Argue

One acceptable
answer

Competing
reasonable answers

ASK

an expert

ENQUIRE

together

Where is the world's most remote
island?

Would cutting themselves off from
the outside world be better?

Our World

Provoked by the story but going
beyond it

Exploring questions 3

SESSION OBJECTIVES

To investigate how questions can help us explore a theme and find out information.

SESSION OUTCOMES

✓ A list of questions that you would ask the people in the picture to find out what had happened and why.

✓ A picture can tell a story, however questions allow a deeper understanding of what may be happening.

LESSON PLAN

➢ Ask the children to remember a time when they observed their class parent understand what their baby wanted without the baby talking.

➢ Discuss how they thought the parent was able to understand and know about their baby.

For those classrooms not able to undertake the Circles for Learning Project, video clips or photographs can be used to support the discussion around the topic and stimulate thoughts and ideas from the children and young people.

Task

KS1: To create a list of questions to ask the people in the picture to find out more about what was happening and why.

KS2/KS3: To use the Question Quadrant to explore and think about the picture in more detail.

KS1

1. Share a picture with the class and discuss what they can see happening.

2. Ask the class to come up with a questions to ask the people in the picture or the person talking/painting the picture to enable them to understand more about what was going on.

3. Explain why they think their question is good.

4. Divide the class up into groups

5. Give each group a picture to look at.

6. Ask each group to come up with 5 questions that they could ask the people in the picture or the person who took/created the picture to understand more about what was happening.

7. Share the pictures and questions with the class. The class to choose their favourite question for each picture and explain why.

KS2/3

1. Divide the class into groups and give each group a picture to discuss.

2. Ask the groups to come up with 10 questions in each quadrant of the Question Quadrant.

3. Display the picture and their questions on a table and create an exhibition.

4. Discuss the exhibition and the questions raised.

5. Discuss the different perspectives people can take from a picture which depend on their own experience. Questions can help clarify understanding.

6. Ask each young person to choose their favourite question from the exhibition and state why they choose it.

7. Ask the young people to choose one question from the Ask the expert section and find the answer for homework.

RESOURCES

1. A selection of pictures (newspaper pictures can be very good)

2. Pens, pencils

3. Paper

4. Sticky notes

5. Question Quadrant for each group

IMPORTANT POINTS

- Questions help us find out more information about something.

- A picture can be interpreted by different people in different ways. Asking questions allows us to understand things better.

LEARNING LINKS

Speaking and listening, collaboration, information processing, questioning, observation.

REFLECTION

Questions:

Positive comment from child:

Positive comment from adult:

LEARNING DIMENSIONS		SOCIAL & EMOTIONAL SKILLS	
Strategic awareness	▓	Emotional literacy	
Learning relationships		Neuroscience	
Curiosity	▓	Self-regulation	
Creativity		Self-development	▓
Meaning making	▓		
Changing & learning	▓		
Resilience			

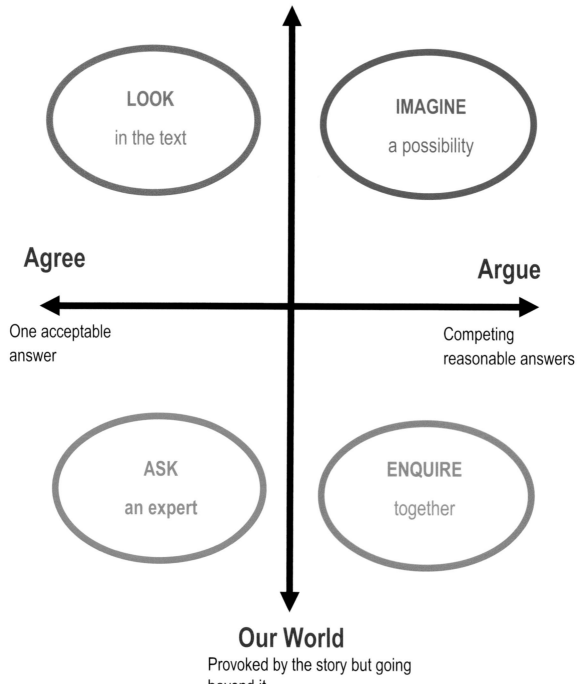

About the characters or story

Stimulus/Story World

LOOK

in the text

IMAGINE

a possibility

Agree

Argue

One acceptable
answer

Competing
reasonable answers

ASK

an expert

ENQUIRE

together

Our World
Provoked by the story but going
beyond it

The Why Ladder

SESSION OBJECTIVES

To explore and deepen our knowledge of how questions can extend our understanding of information, ideas and situations.

SESSION OUTCOMES

✓ To create a Why Ladder of linking questions that increase our understanding of an area.

LESSON PLAN

➤ Ask the children to remember a time when their class baby was asking questions.

➤ Discuss what they were trying to understand and why.

For those classrooms not able to undertake the Circles for Learning Project, video clips or photographs can be used to support the discussion around the topic and stimulate thoughts and ideas from the children and young people.

Task

KS1: To work as a group to complete a collection of questions linked with a chosen topic.
KS2/KS3: To work in pairs to create a Why Ladder.

KS1

1. Working as a class, ask a child to choose a question from a bowl.

2. Share the question with the class – give them the answer and then ask them to think of another related question. E.g. Q. Why do we have money? A. So we can buy things from each other. Q. How is money made? A. Money is made at the Royal Mint. Q. Why is the

Queen's Head on our money? A. So that we know it is legal and not fake. Q. Is the Queen on everyone's money?

3. Put the children into small groups and give them a topic to think of questions around. Stick the question in the middle of a large piece of paper. They can draw or write there question around the paper.

4. Share what each group has done.

KS2/3

1. Share a Why Ladder with the children and young people.

2. Divide the class into small groups.

3. Ask each group to make up a question for the box.

4. Ask the groups to choose a question from the box. They have one pass if they do not like the question.

5. Ask them to complete the Question Ladder as far as they can.

6. Share the ladders created.

RESOURCES

1. Question slips

2. Question Ladder

3. Question Quadrant

4. Why, What, When, Where, How question headings

5. Computers/internet for research of questions

IMPORTANT POINTS

Questions enable us to expand and clarify what we know.

LEARNING LINKS

Speaking and listening, enquiry, literacy, working together, general knowledge.

REFLECTION

Questions:

Positive comment from child:

Positive comment from adult:

LEARNING DIMENSIONS		SOCIAL & EMOTIONAL SKILLS	
Strategic awareness		Emotional literacy	
Learning relationships		Neuroscience	
Curiosity		Self-regulation	
Creativity		Self-development	
Meaning making			
Changing & learning			
Resilience			

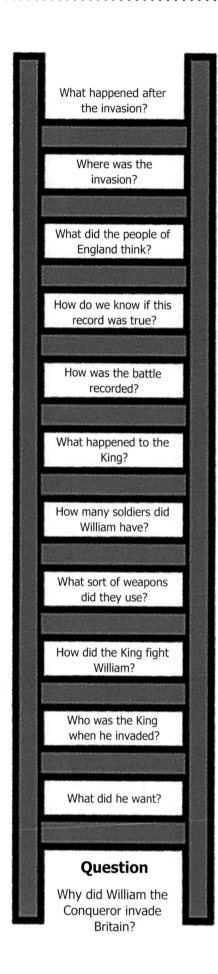

What happened after
the invasion?

Where was the
invasion?

What did the people of
England think?

How do we know if this
record was true?

How was the battle
recorded?

What happened to the
King?

How many soldiers did
William have?

What sort of weapons
did they use?

How did the King fight
William?

Who was the King
when he invaded?

What did he want?

Question

Why did William the
Conqueror invade
Britain?

Why do I have to go to school?	Why do we have money?
Can a blind person read?	What is climate change?
How is a pencil made?	Who invented writing?
Where is the tallest building in the world?	Which country in the world is the largest?
What is the most poisonous snake in the world?	What is deforestation?
Do plants die of old age?	Can germs catch germs?
How many bones are there in a human skeleton?	Why do we have bad dreams?
Why is sleep good for us?	What are hiccups?
Do other animals get allergies?	Do blind people see in their dreams?

Risk-friendly climate

SESSION OBJECTIVES

To discuss and then create a Risk-friendly Classroom Climate Charter.

SESSION OUTCOMES

✓ To explore what we need to have a friendly classroom where we can take risks in our learning.

✓ To discuss, agree and then create a Risk-friendly Classroom Climate Charter.

LESSON PLAN

➤ Ask the children to recall a time when they watched their class baby look to their parent for help or support.

➤ Discuss what the baby needed to experience so that they could look to their parent for support and help.

➤ Introduce the 'Secure Base' concept of Bowlby's and share this with the children.

For those classrooms not able to undertake the Circles for Learning Project, video clips or photographs can be used to support the discussion around the topic and stimulate thoughts and ideas from the children and young people.

Task

KS1: To create a picture and short caption about being brave when we are learning.
KS2/KS3 To create a Risk-friendly Classroom Charter.

KS1

1. Discuss with the class things we need to be able to learn well and things that can stop us from learning or trying to learn.

2. List them in two groups – positive ☺ and negative ☹

3. Photocopy the items on the positive list and give them to the children. Ask them to order/ rank them.

4. Share what they come up with and then work with the children to put them into positive sentences – in class we will support people having a go or taking a risk in their learning by being supportive and kind. Turn these into postcards or posters to support learning in the classroom.

KS2/3

1. Share the secure base diagram with the children and talk about how their class baby learns.

2. Ask them to share what they need from people if they are to be brave and have a go at something in class? What do they need from people if they are going to be able to make a mistake and know it is OK? How do they need people to respond if they get something wrong or need to ask for help? How would they like children to treat their class baby when they go to school?

3. Ask the children to work in groups and create a Risk-friendly Classroom Charter to show how people will behave so that learning can happen within the classroom.

4. Share the charters people have created and then choose one sentence from each one to go into the class charter.

RESOURCES

1. Picture of John Bowlby

2. Diagram of a secure base

3. Blank charter

IMPORTANT POINTS

If we feel that we have a safe space to learn then we can take risks and make mistakes.

LEARNING LINKS

Relationships, emotional literacy, learning skills, motivation, taking risks, making mistakes, self-awareness.

REFLECTION

Questions:

Positive comment from child:

Positive comment from adult:

LEARNING DIMENSIONS		SOCIAL & EMOTIONAL SKILLS	
Strategic awareness	▓	Emotional literacy	▓
Learning relationships	▓	Neuroscience	
Curiosity		Self-regulation	
Creativity	▓	Self-development	▓
Meaning Making	▓		
Changing & Learning			
Resilience	▓		

Secure base from which to explore

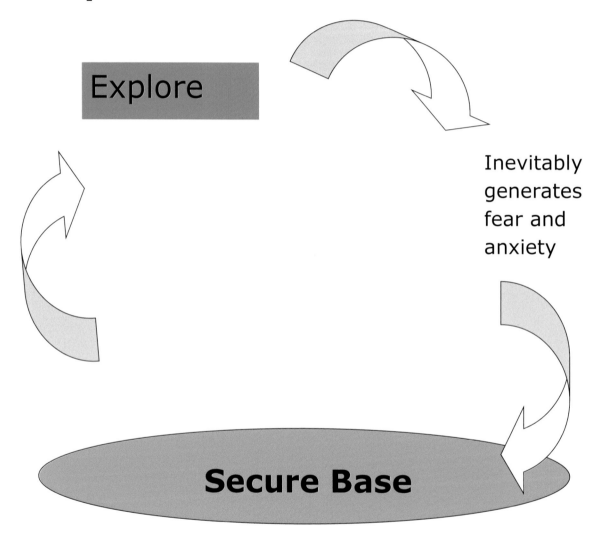

Explore

Inevitably generates fear and anxiety

Secure Base

We look for reassurance and comfort to help us manage how we feel.

New words

SESSION OBJECTIVES

To develop vocabulary in a fun and exciting way.

To increase interest in words.

SESSION OUTCOMES

✓ To create a word wall within the classroom.

✓ To use words to illustrate pictures.

✓ To learn how to play 'Call my Bluff'.

LESSON PLAN

➢ To ask the children to remember a time when their class baby was learning to talk and learning new words. A toddler learns 10 new words every day!

➢ Discuss how they think babies learn new words.

For those classrooms not able to undertake the Circles for Learning Project, video clips or photographs can be used to support the discussion around the topic and stimulate thoughts and ideas from the children and young people.

Task

KS1: To create a word wall.
    To make a new word.
KS2/3: To illustrate a picture with words.
    To play 'Call my Bluff'/'Words in a Minute' and 'Countdown'.

KS1

1. Read the story *Phileas's Fortune* to the children.

2. Explore what they think about the story.

3. Which words do they think would be the most expensive?

4. Which words would they think would be cheap?

5. Divide the children into small groups and give them an envelope of words. Ask the children to give the words they have a value – 1p, 2p, 5p, 10p, 20p, 50p or £1.00. Put the coins on the words.

6. Ask the children to make a sentence with the words – how much is the sentence worth?

7. Share their sentences and their values.

KS2/3

1. Read the story *The Word Collector*.

2. Explore the concept of words changing how people behave or feel.

3. Put the pictures on the desks and ask the children to walk around and write 1 word that could go on each picture.

4. Divide the class into groups and ask each group to choose a picture. Ask the children to fill the picture with words that might make people feel better or change things. E.g. a picture of war – filled with words such as peace, love, friend, support look after, kindness etc.

5. Cut out words from newspapers or magazines and then stick them to the pictures.

6. Share the work in a silent exhibition with the work on desks so the children can walk around and look at each group's words.

RESOURCES

1. *The Word Collector* by Sonja Wimmer

2. *Phileas's Fortune*, a story about self-expression by Agnes de Lestrade and Valeria Docampo

3. Words to give a value to

4. Dictionaries

5. Words in a Minute cards

6. Letters or letter cards

IMPORTANT POINTS

Words have the power to make things better or make things worse.

The words we use towards ourselves in our self-talk has an impact on how we think about ourselves and our feelings and emotions.

LEARNING LINKS

Emotional literacy, literacy, language development, learning relationships, speaking and listening, discussion, negotiation, collaboration.

REFLECTION

Questions:

Positive comment from child:

Positive comment from adult:

LEARNING DIMENSIONS		SOCIAL & EMOTIONAL SKILLS	
Strategic awareness	▓	Emotional literacy	▓
Learning relationships	▓	Neuroscience	
Curiosity		Self-regulation	
Creativity	▓	Self-development	▓
Meaning making			
Changing & learning	▓		
Resilience			

Words of Value

I	play
laugh	fun
sad	happy
cry	angry
my	fields
street	flowers
grass	can
walk	run
sunshine	rain
wind	storm
friend	with
in	sister
brother	Mum
Dad	to
when	love
hate	and
the	

Words in a Minute

Volcanoes	**The brain**
WWII	**The ocean**
Rivers	**Medieval times**
Harry Potter	**The Romans**
Eastenders	**Cars/motorbikes**
Football	**Fashion**
The human body	**The water cycle**
Pollution	**Shapes**
Plants	**School rules**
Artists	**Computers**

Changing and learning

A sense of getting better at learning over time, of growing, changing and adapting as a learner in the whole of life

Different ways of learning

SESSION OBJECTIVES

To understand how we learn.

To understand that different people may learn things in different ways.

SESSION OUTCOMES

✓ To learn a poem.

✓ To be able to discuss with a partner the ways we learnt the poem.

✓ To be able to describe another way that somebody learnt a poem.

LESSON PLAN

➢ Ask the children to remember a time when they watched their class baby learn to do something.

➢ Discuss how they achieved this, did their parent help them? Did they learn by trial and error? Did they learn by watching or copying?

For those classrooms not able to undertake the Circles for Learning Project, video clips or photographs can be used to support the discussion around the topic and stimulate thoughts and ideas from the children and young people.

Task
KS1: To learn a short poem.
KS2/3: To learn a poem.

Learning dimensions

KS1

1. Share with the children something you had to learn – a poem, your tables or a speech.

2. Set the challenge for them to learn a poem.

3. Discuss with the children how they might learn the poem. Help them explore if they have learnt anything before and if so how they did it.

4. Collect the ideas.

5. Choose 3 ideas and try them out over the next few days.

6. When you have finished discuss what you found. Did you all choose the same way of learning? Did some people like different ways?

7. Help the children understand that people are all different and so they learn in different ways. If we want to be a good learner we need to understand the ways we learn.

KS2/3

1. Share with the children something that you have had to learn.

2. Discuss things they have had to learn and the different ways that they achieved this.

3. With each one support the children look at why they liked that way of learning something. When they had used it and how it had worked.

4. Set the challenge to learn a poem.

5. Put children in teams. Each team will learn a verse of the poem in a different way.

6. Activity 1 will learn the verse by listening to it over and over.

   Activity 2 will learn by writing the verse down.

   Activity 3 will learn by reading the verse to themselves.

   Activity 4 will learn by reading the verse, listening to the verse and drawing a picture of what happens and then cutting up the verse and putting it back together.

7. At the end each activity children will write down what they thought and give it a mark out of 3 for Easy, Medium or Difficult.

8. Explore with the children that not only can they choose how to learn something but that different things might need different strategies for them. Making a paper aeroplane – they

may need to watch someone or follow written instructions. Putting a book shelf together they may need to read the instructions or look at the pictures. Cooking – they may need someone to show them.

9. Ask the children/young people to complete the Learning Wheel.

RESOURCES

1. Paper and pens

2. Coloured pens

3. Poem to learn with 4 verses

4. Learning Wheel

IMPORTANT POINTS

•   We learn different things in different ways.

•   We all learn in different ways.

•   I can learn new ways of learning things from others.

LEARNING LINKS

Speaking and listening, collaboration, information processing, questioning, observation, creativity, planning and organisation, teamwork.

REFLECTION

Questions:

Positive comment from child:

Positive comment from adult:

Learning dimensions

LEARNING DIMENSIONS		SOCIAL & EMOTIONAL SKILLS	
Strategic awareness	▓	Emotional literacy	▓
Learning relationships		Neuroscience	
Curiosity		Self-regulation	
Creativity		Self-development	▓
Meaning making			
Changing & learning	▓		
Resilience			

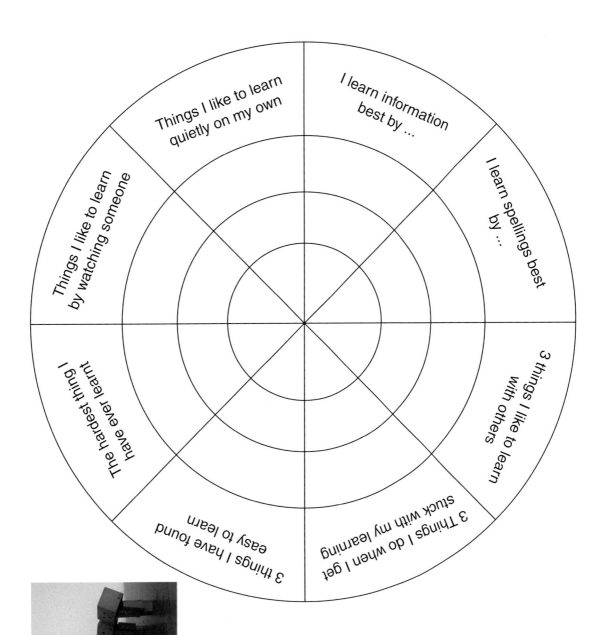

The wheel contains the following sections:

- Things I like to learn quietly on my own
- I learn information best by …
- I learn spellings best by …
- 3 things I like to learn with others
- 3 Things I do when I get stuck with my learning
- 3 things I have found easy to learn
- The hardest thing I have ever learnt
- Things I like to learn by watching someone

Learning Wheel

Milestones

SESSION OBJECTIVES

To create a development timeline.

SESSION OUTCOMES

✓ To understand the word 'milestones'.

✓ A Developmental Milestone Timeline.

LESSON PLAN

➢ Ask the children to think about all the different things their class baby has learnt to do.

➢ Try and put them in order with the baby's age.

For those classrooms not able to undertake the Circles for Learning Project, video clips or photographs can be used to support the discussion around the topic and stimulate thoughts and ideas from the children and young people.

Task

KS1: To put the pictures of a bay doing things in order.

KS2: To put the list of things a baby has learnt to do in order and then find the ages that a baby/toddler would learn to do these things.

KS3: Create a time line for themselves and show the things that they have learnt and at what ages.

KS1

1. Introduce important word – 'milestones' – and discuss definition with the children.

2. Recap on what their class baby has learnt to do with their talking partners and then share with the class.

3. As a group place these statements in order.

4. Ask the best way to record these milestones? Suggest a timeline – draw this out for the children and put in the months/years.

5. Give children new pictures in groups can they agree in which order to place these.

6. Share and discuss.

7. Finish by discussing what they have learnt to do – as they are older.

8. What one thing are they looking forward to being able to do this year? One thing they are looking forward to do in the future?

KS2

1. Introduce important word – 'milestones' – and discuss definition with the children.

2. Recap on what their class baby has learnt to do with their talking partners and then share with the class.

3. As a group place these statements in order.

4. Ask the best way to record these milestones? Suggest a timeline – draw this out for the children and put in the months/years

5. Ask the children to place the statements on their timeline in the correct order and under the correct month/year.

6. Share and discuss what they have found.

7. Remind the children that they have done all this and much more.

8. Ask the children what they are looking forward to learning this year and also in the future.

KS3

1. Introduce important word – 'milestones' – and discuss definition with the children.

2. Recap on what their class baby has learnt to do with their talking partners and then share with the class.

3. As a group place the things their baby has learnt to do in order.

4. Ask the young people to draw their own time line and show all the things that they have learnt to do – walking, riding a bike, cooking, texting etc.

5. Share what they have come up with – how many things have they learnt how to do?

6. What are they looking forward to learning in the future?

RESOURCES

1. Pictures of babies doing things – developmental pictures – walking sitting, crawling, eating, breast feeding, rolling over, talking, etc.

2. Developmental milestone timeline.

IMPORTANT POINTS

Introduce Amazing Baby Facts, such as:

- Baby could tell who Mum is by smell after day 1

- Baby knew Mum's voice and could turn head to find Mum after day 1.

LEARNING LINKS

Speaking and listening, collaboration, empathy, information processing, questioning, science.

REFLECTION

Questions:

Positive comment from child:

Positive comment from adult:

LEARNING DIMENSIONS		SOCIAL & EMOTIONAL SKILLS	
Strategic awareness	▓	Emotional Literacy	
Learning relationships		Neuroscience	
Curiosity		Self-regulation	
Creativity		Self-development	▓
Meaning making			
Changing & learning	▓		
Resilience			

Crying means that a baby can get help from an adult.	**Turn their head from side to side.**
Eyes open and can see things close up.	**Can hear sounds noises and voices.**
A baby starts talking with coos and gurgles.	**A baby starts to smile when she/ he is happy or pleased.**
Playing with her/ his hands and feet.	**Trying to grab things that are held out for her/ him**
Trying out new noises – squealing, and other sounds. Mama, dada	**Able to roll over from back to tummy and tummy to back.**
Can sit up if supported by an adult.	**Trying special solid baby foods.**
Testing out their legs by standing if supported by an adult.	**See things further away now – across a room.**

Playing with objects and feeling them in their mouth.	**Sitting up unsupported.**
Starting to crawl or bottom shuffle and can get around.	**Pick up objects with her thumb and finger.**
Hold things for themselves – bottle or beaker	**Pull themselves up on furniture and stand for a short time.**
Walk around the room supported by furniture.	**Say their first word.**
Walk unaided. Pick up a small object and put it into a container.	**Wave goodbye. First tooth is through.**
Pick up an object and give it to someone.	

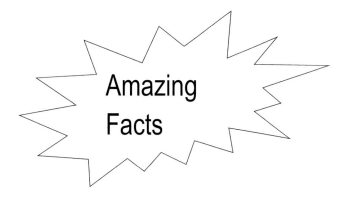

Amazing
Facts

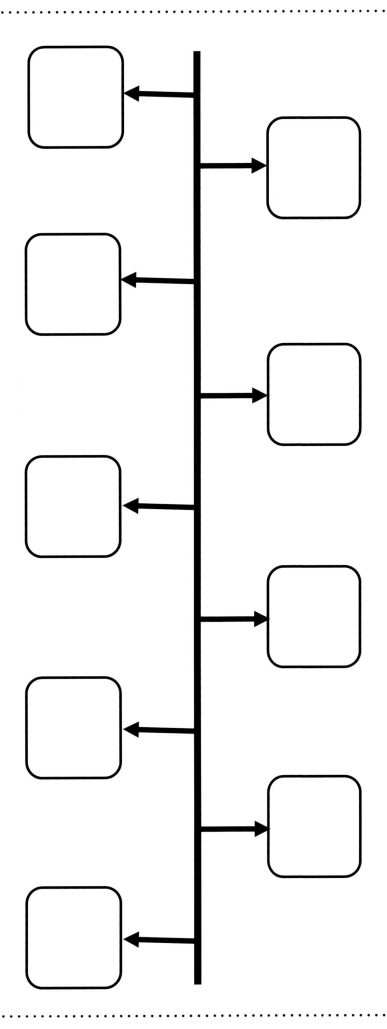

My learning toolkit/What are my learning strategies?

SESSION OBJECTIVES

To identify my own ways of learning and to understand that I use different learning strategies for different things.

SESSION OUTCOMES

✓ My learning thoughts and feelings narrative.

✓ My Learning Journal film strip.

✓ A list of learning strategies I have mastered.

LESSON PLAN

➢ Ask the children to think of all the things that their class baby has learnt to do since they have been observing them.

➢ Remind the children that as a toddler their class baby is learning 10 new words a day.

➢ Remind the children of all the social interactions and the learning environment that their class baby is encountering and how this causes the neurons to fire and make connections in the brain.

For those classrooms not able to undertake the Circles for Learning Project, video clips or photographs can be used to support the discussion around the topic and stimulate thoughts and ideas from the children and young people.

Task

KS1: To learn to count to 10 in another language.

KS2: To make an origami animal.

KS3: To learn a card trick.

KS1

1. Discuss with the children something that you have recently learnt to do.

2. Explain to them that you are going to teach them to count to 10 in another language.

3. Explain that you are going to record how they learn, what they think and what they feel as they undertake the learning task.

4. Count to 10 in the new language and record what their immediate thoughts were.

    I can't do this, wow this is fun, I know some of these already etc.

5. As they are working stop at different points to record how they feel and the thoughts they are having. Show this on a time graph to help children see how the thinking and feelings change as they work.

KS2

1. Discuss with the children something that you have recently learnt to do.

2. Discuss strategies you used to support your learning and being able to achieve what you set out to do.

3. Explain that you are going to learn something together and create your own Learning Journey diagram.

4. Share the origami pictures with the children and ask them to choose one of them. Then complete the Learning Journey film strip individually. The children can choose to

    *   Phone a friend or work with a partner

    *   Work with a group of others

    *   Ask for help from an expert

    *   Use the online visual support

    If they choose any of these then they have to state why they needed to, what they were feeling before and after, how it helped and what they have learned by using this strategy.

5. When the children have finished making the origami animal and their learning journal filmstrip share the different experiences.

6. Discuss what they have learnt about learning and about themselves as a learner.

KS3

1. Discuss with the children something that you have recently learnt to do.

2. Discuss strategies you used to support your learning and being able to achieve what you set out to do.

3. Explain that you are going to learn something together and create your own Learning Journey diagram.

4. Working in pairs, ask the children to research how to do a card trick on the internet.

5. Practise together until they are able to do the trick. Record how they felt, what they were thinking and how the learning was going.

6. Share the trick with another pair.

7. Discuss the journey that they went on to learn the card trick – Was it easy? How did they keep going when it went wrong? What made them keep going? What was the internal self-talk that they used to keep themselves focused?

RESOURCES

1. Video clip or numbers in another language

2. Learning Journey film strip

3. Selection of origami paper

4. Selection of origami instructions to make animals

5. A selection of card tricks – videos or instructions

6. Learning Journey timeline example

IMPORTANT POINTS

- Understanding and celebrating the strategies we have already developed for learning.

- Experiencing that there are many learning strategies available to us that we can use for different learning.

LEARNING LINKS

Speaking and listening, collaboration, information processing, questioning, observation, creativity.

REFLECTION

Questions:

Positive comment from child:

Positive comment from adult:

LEARNING DIMENSIONS		SOCIAL & EMOTIONAL SKILLS	
Strategic awareness	▓	Emotional literacy	
Learning relationships		Neuroscience	
Curiosity		Self-regulation	
Creativity		Self-development	▓
Meaning making			
Changing & learning	▓		
Resilience			

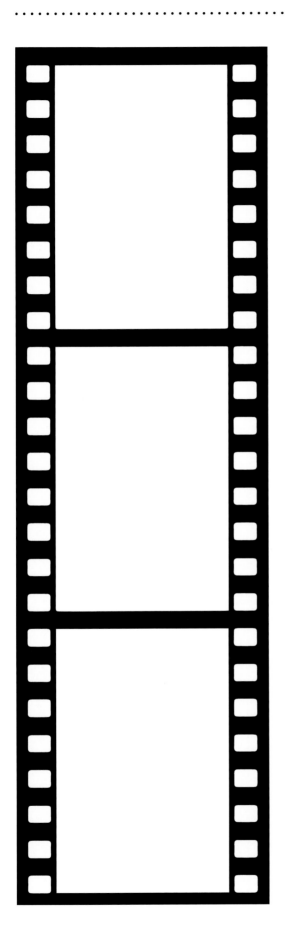

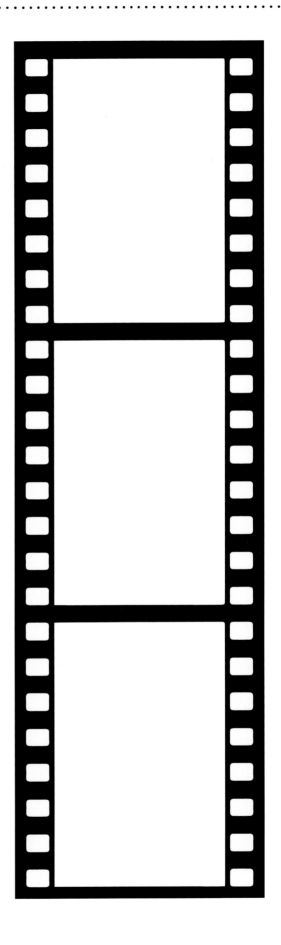

Learning Journey Timeline Example

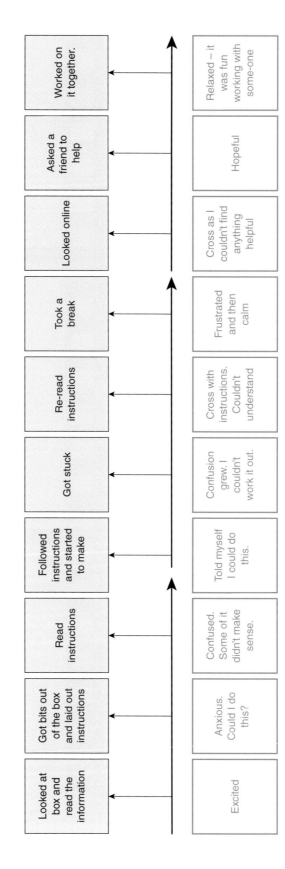

ACTIONS

| Looked at box and read the information | Got bits out of the box and laid out instructions | Read instructions | Followed instructions and started to make | Got stuck | Re-read instructions | Took a break | Looked online | Asked a friend to help | Worked on it together. |

EMOTIONS

| Excited | Anxious. Could I do this? | Confused. Some of it didn't make sense. | Told myself I could do this. | Confusion grew. I couldn't work it out. | Cross with instructions. Couldn't understand | Frustrated and then calm | Cross as I couldn't find anything helpful | Hopeful | Relaxed – it was fun working with some-one |

Look what I can do now!

SESSION OBJECTIVES

To celebrate the things I have learnt to do.

SESSION OUTCOMES

✓ How I think about my abilities to learn impacts on how I learn.

✓ To celebrate all the things I have already learnt to do.

✓ To share the things I am looking forward to being able to do.

LESSON PLAN

➢ Remind the children of all the social interactions and the learning environment that their class baby is encountering and how this causes the neurons to fire and make connections in the brain.

For those classrooms not able to undertake the Circles for Learning Project, video clips or photographs can be used to support the discussion around the topic and stimulate thoughts and ideas from the children and young people.

Task
KS1: To create a timeline to show the things that they have learnt to do since they were born.
KS2/KS3: To learn a magic trick.

KS1
1. Ask the children to list all the things they have learnt to do since they were born.

2. Ask each child to draw one of the things.

3. Photocopy so that you have a selection of small pictures showing something that the children have learnt.

4. Ask the children to choose one thing for each year and stick it on their timeline.

5. Ask them to draw three things that they are looking forward to learning over the next few years and add them to their timeline.

KS2/3

1. Ask the children to research a magic trick and then learn to do this. This has to be a new one and cannot be one that they already know.

2. Divide the children into pairs and ask them to interview their partner about what it was like to learn this trick. Use interview questions: What was the easiest part of learning the trick? How did you keep yourself going when the trick didn't work at the beginning? What was the self-talk you used when trying to learn how to do the trick? How did it feel when you were first able to do it without a mistake? Etc.

3. Ask the children to take this information and create a Learning Profile of their partner. This could be a poster, a letter introducing them to their new Head Teacher. This could include: Tom enjoys a challenge; he is able to keep himself motivated even when the learning becomes difficult; Tom has a variety of positive self-talk strategies that he uses to keep himself going when learning and is well motivated to achieve his goal; Tom can find sharing the strategies he uses difficult, however with support he is able to recognise themn and share them with others.

4. Correlate all the information and create a graph to show the feedback from the class.

RESOURCES

1. Blank timeline

2. Interview questions

IMPORTANT POINTS

• Understanding and celebrating the strategies we have already developed for learning.

LEARNING LINKS

Speaking and listening, collaboration, information processing, questioning, observation, creativity.

REFLECTION:

Questions:

Positive comment from child:

Positive comment from adult:

LEARNING DIMENSIONS		SOCIAL & EMOTIONAL SKILLS	
Strategic awareness		Emotional literacy	
Learning relationships		Neuroscience	
Curiosity		Self-regulation	
Creativity		Self-development	
Meaning making			
Changing & learning			
Resilience			

QUESTIONS	ANSWERS
1. What is the hardest thing you have ever learnt to do?	
2. What strategies did you use to achieve this?	
3. What are you most proud of having learnt?	
4. What are you looking most forward to learning in the future?	
5. What 3 strategies do you use when the learning becomes difficult?	
6. What strategy do you use when you become frustrated by your learning?	
7. Which skills in a teacher do you appreciate most when you are struggling with your learning?	
8. Which is your favourite way of learning a. Watching b. Being told how to do something c. Following written instructions d. Being allowed to work it out for yourself.	
9. What sort of environment do you like best for learning?	

QUESTIONS	ANSWERS
10. Do you think you are good at learning?	
11. Out of school, who is the best person to teach you things? What makes them so good?	
12. Who do you think is the best person at learning that you know? Why?	

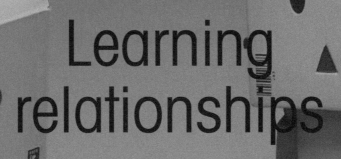

Learning relationships

Learning with and from others, and also being able to manage without them

Create an advert to celebrate who you are and what you can do

SESSION OBJECTIVES

To identify our characteristics and celebrate how unique we all are.

SESSION OUTCOMES

✓ An advert/poster to celebrate ourselves.

✓ To understand that we are all different and unique which means we are all special.

LESSON PLAN

➤ Ask the children to remember a time when their class parent labelled their class baby in a positive way.

➤ Discuss how these labels build up over time and support the baby have an idea of themselves

➤ Ask them to say what they love about their class baby. Look at the many different aspects people see.

For those classrooms not able to undertake the Circles for Learning Project, video clips or photographs can be used to support the discussion around the topic and stimulate thoughts and ideas from the children and young people.

. . . .

Task

KS1: To create picture of their friend and put things that they are good at or that people like about them around the picture.

KS2/3: To create a personal advert for their friend or video advert.

KS1

1. Ask the children to choose a stone from the basket that they like.

2. Share with each other why they had chosen the stone.

3. Discuss the fact that each stone is different and is beautiful to different people in different ways.

4. Pair up the children and ask them to draw a picture of their partner in the middle of a piece of paper (A3).

5. Lay the pieces of paper out on the table in small groups (6 to a table) ask the groups to go around the pictures and write on a sticky note something that each person was good at and 1 thing that they liked about the person.

6. Each person who drew a picture adds the sticky notes or writes what they have to say on the picture.

7. Meet in a circle and exchange the pictures so that the children can see what people liked or thought about them.

8. Display them in class under a title – Let's Celebrate How Amazing We All Are.

KS2/3

1. Ask the children to choose a stone from the basket that they like.

2. Share with each other why they had chosen the stone.

3. Discuss the fact that each stone is different and is beautiful to different people in different ways.

4. Pair up the children and ask them to draw a picture of their partner in the middle of a piece of paper (A3).

5. Then write questions that would help them find out about their partner so that they can create a 'Person Advert' to celebrate them.

6. Recap on questions and how they are able to help us gather more information and then 'drill down' to really find out what a person thinks feels or believes.

. . . .

7. Pairs to ask their questions and then write statement under their questions on their poster draft.

8. Use their draft poster to complete their advert.

9. Alternatively, film adverts could be created to show off the person and their unique qualities. The partner could introduce the candidate and talk about them while the candidate is filmed in the background doing a range of different activities or showing their skills.

RESOURCES

1. Basket of stones

2. Sticky notes

3. Paper and pens

4. Tablet computers

5. Adverts

IMPORTANT POINTS

• Understanding and celebrating ourselves.

• Using questions to gather more information.

LEARNING LINKS

Speaking and listening, collaboration, information processing, questioning, observation, creativity.

REFLECTION

Questions:

Positive comment from child:

Positive comment from adult:

LEARNING DIMENSIONS		SOCIAL & EMOTIONAL SKILLS	
Strategic awareness		Emotional literacy	
Learning relationships		Neuroscience	
Curiosity		Self-regulation	
Creativity	▓	Self-development	▓
Meaning making			
Changing & learning			
Resilience			

The build a brain team challenge

SESSION OBJECTIVES

To develop a greater understanding of the brain.

To develop skills of collaboration and teamwork.

SESSION OUTCOMES

✓ A brain showing different areas that are responsible for different things.

✓ A completed Team Project.

LESSON PLAN

➢ Ask the children to remember a time when their class baby and parent had to work together.

➢ Discuss the skills used by the adult to make this successful.

For those classrooms not able to undertake the Circles for Learning Project, video clips or photographs can be used to support the discussion around the topic and stimulate thoughts and ideas from the children and young people.

Task

KS1: Working in pairs create a model of a brain.
KS2: Working in small groups create a model of a brain.
KS3: Working in small groups create a rough idea of an advert to pitch to the manufacturers of the Neuro Brain 3000.

Learning dimensions

KS1/2

1. Group the children in teams of 2, 4 or 6.

2. Show them the 'NEW Neuro Brain Poster'. Set the challenge – to make a model Neuro Brain 3000. Explain that they have 50 min to make the Neuro 3000 and that it has to include all the areas described in the advert.

3. Explain that the brain must fulfil the following brief:

    • Be the size of a human head.

    • Show the thought waves paths.

    • Have an area of creativity.

    • Have an emotional area.

    • Have an imagination area.

    • Have an area for generating weird and wacky thoughts.

    • Have a FUN generating area.

    • Have a socket to connect to the outside world.

4. When the 50 min is up, ask the children to display their brains on a table.

5. Ask them to see how well each brain has met its brief.

6. Discuss how the team worked – explore what positive strategies were needed and how they made people feel.

7. Identify negative ways of working and explain how they made people feel.

KS2/3

1. Group the children in teams of 2, 4 or 6.

2. Show them the 'NEW Neuro Brain Poster'. Set the challenge – to create a presentation to the manufacturers of the Neuro Brain 3000 to try to get the job of making the advert.

3. Explain that the brain has been designed to:

    • Be the size of a human head.
    • Show the thought waves paths.

- Have an area of creativity.
- Have an emotional area.
- Have an imagination area.
- Have an area for generating weird and wacky thoughts.
- Have a FUN generating area.
- Have a socket to connect to the outside world.

4. When they have completed the task ask them to present to the class.

5. Create a panel of judges – one person from each team who needs to give the presentation a mark out of 10 (as in *Strictly Come Dancing*).

6. Discuss how the teams functioned – what are good teamwork strategies/behaviours/ways of behaving and how did they make people feel? What are negative strategies/ways of behaving/interacting when working in a team?

RESOURCES

1. Model of a brain

2. Examples of advertisement presentations:

   https://www.youtube.com/watch?v=U6H5j3FkIHA
   https://www.youtube.com/watch?v=dEDccOaCjaA

3. Sticky notes

4. Paper and pens

5. Coloured pens

6. Junk for junk modelling

7. Modelling clay

8. Collage materials

9. Paint

10. Glue

11. Newspaper

12. Balloons, pipe cleaners, sticky tape

13. Timer/clock

IMPORTANT POINTS

- Teamwork.

- Different parts of the brain are responsible for different things.

LEARNING LINKS

Speaking and listening, collaboration, information processing, questioning, observation, creativity, planning and organisation, teamwork.

REFLECTION

Questions:

Positive comment from child:

Positive comment from adult:

LEARNING DIMENSIONS		SOCIAL & EMOTIONAL SKILLS	
Strategic awareness		Emotional literacy	▩
Learning relationships	▩	Neuroscience	
Curiosity		Self-regulation	
Creativity	▩	Self-development	▩
Meaning making			
Changing & learning	▩		
Resilience			

Think faster than ever with

The NEW Neuro 3000

• Special creativity area

• Larger emotional area

• Faster imagination

• NEW wacky thoughts area

• Exciting FUN generation area

• New reliable socket to connect to the outside world when you need to.

• Shows brighter thought waves paths than ever before

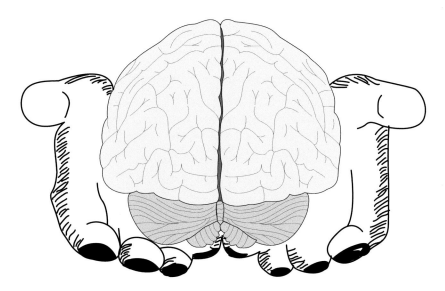

Less warm up time, faster problem solving makes school life easy and bad homework nights a thing of the past.
Yours for just $6000

What is teamwork?

SESSION OBJECTIVES

To identify ways of behaving/interacting that are conducive to the ability to work in groups.

SESSION OUTCOMES

✓ To create a list of positive behaviours/ strategies/ways of being that support teamwork.

✓ To create a good teamwork description.

LESSON PLAN

➢ Ask the children to remember a time when they watcher people working as a team.

➢ Ask them to describe what they noticed and why they think this made the team work well.

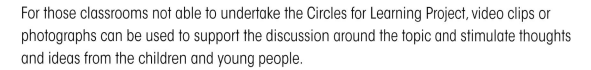

For those classrooms not able to undertake the Circles for Learning Project, video clips or photographs can be used to support the discussion around the topic and stimulate thoughts and ideas from the children and young people.

Task

KS1: To identify 3 things that people can do that help you when you are working in a group.
KS2: To create a list of positive and negative ways of behaving/attitudes/strategies when working with others in a team.
KS3: Create a poster that shows positive ways of behaving/strategies/attitudes that enable teamwork to be successful for all.

KS1

1. Ask the children to remember the work they did on creating the Neuro 3000 brain and what it was like to work in a team.

2. Identify the behaviours and ways of being that they found helpful from others.

3. Read the book *Teamwork Isn't My Thing* by Julia Cook.

4. Discuss the book and the advice the coach gave.

5. Ask the children to draw one piece of advice that they believe is important when working in a team – listen to others, be positive, share your ideas etc.

6. Create a display showing the many different ways of being a team member.

KS2

1. Read the book *Teamwork Isn't My Thing* by Julia Cook.

2. Divide the children into groups and ask them to create a list of good advice for working in a team and things that are not useful when working in a team.

3. Share these ideas as a class and discuss what it is like when people don't listen to your ideas – how does it make you feel? Or when you are included and people encourage you. Explore the impact of behaviour and the team outcome.

4. Ask each child to create a double-page spread showing how certain behaviour makes them feel and giving the alternative.

KS3

1. Ask the children to define teamwork and why it is important.

2. In pairs ask them to make a list of positive and negative ways of behaving within a team and the consequences of this behaviour to others.

3. Divide the class into groups and ask them to create a poster to show positive ways of being in a team and how these ways of behaving make others feel.

4. Create an exhibition of work and ask other students to visit and leave comments by each poster as to why they think it is beneficial.

5. Discuss the comments and the ideas.

RESOURCES

1. *Teamwork Isn't My Thing and I Don't Like to Share* by Julia Cook

2. Examples of posters that promote a way of behaving

3. Double page spread on how behaviours make us feel

IMPORTANT POINTS

When we use positive teamwork strategies and ways of behaving the team works well and succeeds in its task.

The way we behave has an impact on others.

LEARNING LINKS

Speaking and listening, working together, collaboration, Literacy, presentation, creativity.

REFLECTION

Questions:

Positive comment from child:

Positive comment from adult:

LEARNING DIMENSIONS		SOCIAL & EMOTIONAL SKILLS	
Strategic awareness	▓	Emotional literacy	
Learning relationships	▓	Neuroscience	
Curiosity		Self-regulation	
Creativity		Self-development	▓
Meaning making	▓		
Changing & learning	▓		
Resilience			

When people listen to what I have to say it makes me feel like part of the team and makes me want to help everyone to succeed.

When people don't listen to my ideas it makes me feel like I don't want to be with them.

Skills for collaboration

SESSION OBJECTIVES

To be able to define collaboration and explain why it is a useful skill to develop.

SESSION OUTCOMES

✓ To create a short video showing children collaborating.

✓ To create a poster of photographs showing collaboration in different situations.

✓ To create a piece of art work to depict collaboration.

LESSON PLAN

➢ Ask the children to imagine what it is like to have a family and support everyone to do the things that need to happen.

➢ Ask if they think one person can do this?

For those classrooms not able to undertake the Circles for Learning Project, video clips or photographs can be used to support the discussion around the topic and stimulate thoughts and ideas from the children and young people.

Task

KS1: To create a whole class display to show collaboration in school.
KS2: To create a short video to demonstrate what collaboration is.
KS3: To create a piece of art work to depict collaboration.

KS1

1. Continue the discussion about families – be careful to enable children to understand that families come in all shapes and sizes and are made of different people. Link families with the classroom.

2. Discuss how everyone needs to support each other and work together to make a family work and that is the same in the classroom and in the school.

3. Ask the children to have a thinking storm to collect ideas of ways that people collaborate in school to help it work well.

4. Make a list of things and then ask the children to photograph them.

5. Create a whole school collaboration display board – showing the many different ways people work together to achieve a happy successful school.

KS2

1. Discuss the word 'collaboration'.

2. Ask the children to have a thinking storm to come up with ideas of how children need to collaborate together.

3. Set the challenge of creating a short video to show the power and importance of collaboration.

4. Divide the class into groups and ask them to produce a photo shoot plan of how their video will look on the film strip.

5. Share their ideas with the class and ask for feedback.

6. Make adjustments according to the feedback.

7. Get them to film their collaboration video.

8. Have a film afternoon with popcorn and share all the videos.

9. Present the best film with an Oscar.

KS3

1. Divide the class into small groups.

2. Ask each group to find a definition, different examples and a picture that shows collaboration.

3. Share what they have found.

4. Discuss the different findings.

5. Ask each group to create a piece of art work to depict collaboration.

6. Hold an exhibition and share the different pieces of art.

RESOURCES

1. Tablet computers

2. Art materials

3. Large paper

4. Access to the internet

5. Paint

6. Pens and coloured pencils

7. Pastels and chalks

8. Clay

9. Access to computers

IMPORTANT POINTS

Collaboration means everyone taking part to achieve something. The classroom and school need all people to collaborate for it to function fully.

We all have a part to play in collaboration.

LEARNING LINKS

Speaking and listening, planning and organisation, creativity, working together.

REFLECTION

Questions:

Positive comment from child:

Positive comment from adult:

LEARNING DIMENSIONS		SOCIAL & EMOTIONAL SKILLS	
Strategic awareness	▩	Emotional literacy	
Learning relationships	▩	Neuroscience	
Curiosity		Self-regulation	
Creativity		Self-development	▩
Meaning making			
Changing & learning	▩		
Resilience			

Constructive feedback

SESSION OBJECTIVES

To understand the importance of making feedback constructive.

To understand that constructive feedback helps us to become better at something.

SESSION OUTCOMES

✓ To be able to give another child feedback on a piece of work.

✓ To be able to describe what constructive feedback should be like and how it should make the learner feel.

LESSON PLAN

➤ Ask the children to think of a time when they watched their class parent coach/support their class baby to achieve something.

➤ Discuss the words they used and their tone of voice.

➤ Help the children think about how hard it is to allow their class baby to struggle and do something for themselves and not to do it for them.

For those classrooms not able to undertake the Circles for Learning Project, video clips or photographs can be used to support the discussion around the topic and stimulate thoughts and ideas from the children and young people.

Task

KS1: To be able to tell another child what they like about the piece of work they have done, what they wish they could do next time, what they wonder would happen if…

KS2/3: To be able to give constructive feedback using the 'I like, I wish and I wonder' format.
To be able to use appropriate tone of voice and body language to deliver the feedback.

KS1

1. Working with another adult demonstrate feedback about a piece of work in a negative way.

2. Discuss with the children how the person was made to feel.

3. Was this helpful for their learning?

4. Ask the children to work in pairs and come up with another way of giving feedback.

5. Share their role play.

6. After each one ask the children to identify the strategies that they used – kind tone of voice, thoughtful facial expressions, positive and negative statements etc.

7. Introduce the 'I like, I wish, I wonder' statements and discuss what the children think.

8. Create a list of do's and don'ts when giving feedback to others.

KS2/3

1. Discuss what it is like to get feedback on a piece of work and how this can make you feel.

2. Discuss and clarify the point of feedback to another person.

3. Divide the children up into small groups and set the challenge – to demonstrate giving feedback to a group of children and young people from a different country where this has never happened.

4. Ask them to create a do's and don'ts list as a crib sheet to use.

5. Discuss what they have come up with and agree on a list.

RESOURCES

1. 'I like, I wish, I wonder' poster

2. Pictures of coaches working with students

3. Work to share

4. Do's and don'ts sheet

IMPORTANT POINTS

The reason for giving constructive feedback is to enable the student to get better at something.

LEARNING LINKS

Learning relationships, speaking and listening, skills for learning.

REFLECTION

Questions:

Positive comment from child:

Positive comment from adult:

LEARNING DIMENSIONS		SOCIAL & EMOTIONAL SKILLS	
Strategic awareness	▓	Emotional literacy	
Learning relationships	▓	Neuroscience	
Curiosity		Self-regulation	
Creativity		Self-development	▓
Meaning making	▓		
Changing & learning	▓		
Resilience			

Learning dimensions

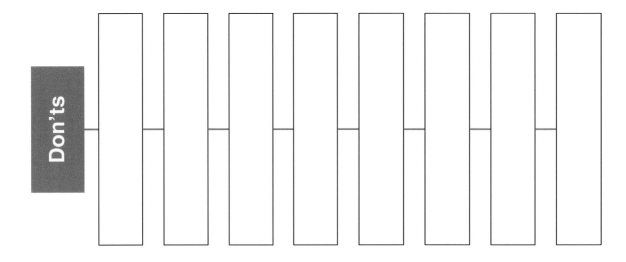

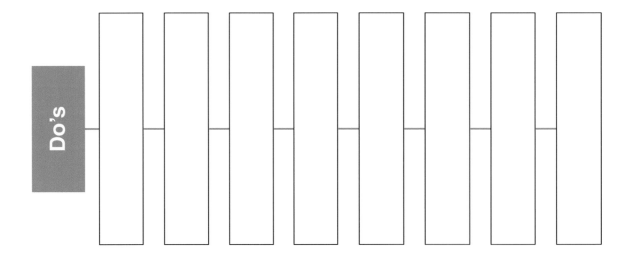

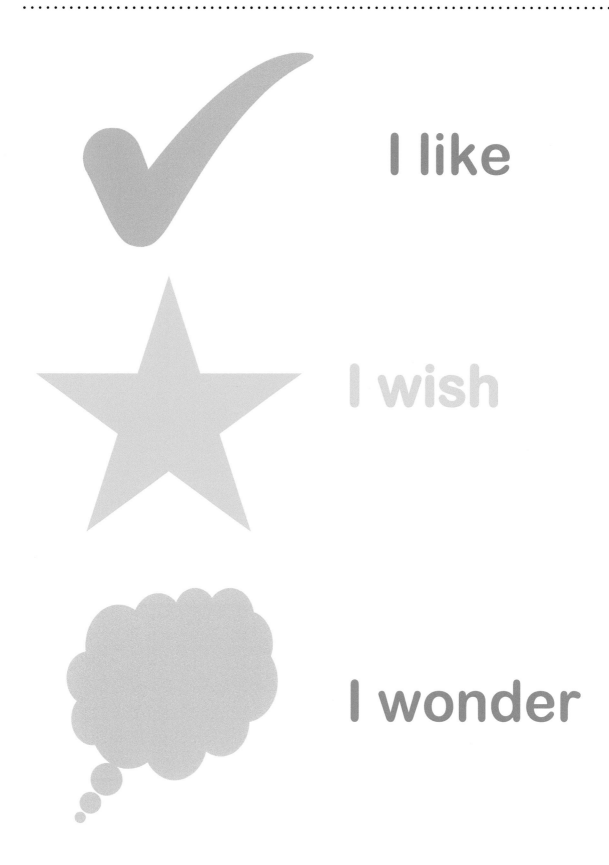

I like

I wish

I wonder

Meaning making

*Making
connections
and seeing
that learning
matters to me*

Before baby arrives

SESSION OBJECTIVES

To investigate how we learn to socialise (be with others) and learn.

SESSION OUTCOMES

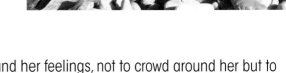

✓ A Mind Map® about 'What we know about babies already' and 'What we would like to know.'

✓ Set of ground rules for the sessions.

- To be thoughtful about baby, not to shout or make loud noises that might frighten her.

- To treat baby gently, not touching her unless her parent says it is OK.

- To be careful and respectful of baby and her feelings, not to crowd around her but to give her and her parent space.

LESSON PLAN

For those classrooms not able to undertake the Circles for Learning Project, video clips or photographs can be used to support the discussion around the topic and stimulate thoughts and ideas from the children and young people.

Task
KS1/2: To create a class Mind Map showing what we know about babies and what we would like to know.

To create a list of rules we will follow when the class baby and their parent visit our classroom.
1. Explain to the children the journey we are going to go on. Talk to the children about baby and parent coming into school and the work we will be doing over the next term.

2. Class thinking storm. Find out what we know about babies already. What do you think they can do, eat or understand? Put this on a large Mind Map on the wall.

3. In partners think about questions we would like to ask mum when she comes into school. Add these to the Mind Map.

4. Discuss questions that they have about babies and add these to the Mind Map.

5. As a class choose the top 10 questions to ask Mum/Dad when they come into class.

6. Discuss their role when baby and parent come in – to observe and watch what happens. The question at the end will be:

    'What did you notice and why was that interesting?'

    'What did you find out that you didn't know before?'

    'What questions has it made you want to find out?'

    'What would you like to find out more about?'

7. Ask the children what they think visiting the class will be like for their class baby. How will they feel? What might they need? What would we need to do?

8. Support the discussion to enable the children to create a list of rules to follow when their baby and parent visit.

9. Ensure that hygiene is discussed and that the children think about what to put on the floor, any toys they give the baby to play with and how to wash their hands.

RESOURCES

1. Large wall display to write Mind Map on

2. Pens for flip chart

3. Photos of a baby

IMPORTANT POINTS

*   Babies cry when there is a problem – it is for the adult to try and problem-solve what that might be and to put it right.

*   The baby's relationship with their parent is very important – they are dependent on them for survival.

LEARNING LINKS

Speaking and listening, collaboration, empathy, information processing, questioning, observation.

REFLECTION

Questions:

Positive comment from child:

Positive comment from adult:

LEARNING DIMENSIONS		SOCIAL & EMOTIONAL SKILLS	
Strategic awareness		Emotional literacy	
Learning relationships		Neuroscience	
Curiosity		Self-regulation	
Creativity		Self-development	
Meaning making			
Changing & learning			
Resilience			

Let's relax

SESSION OBJECTIVES

To learn that the brain and body both need regular focused down time to be able to work and learn effectively.

SESSION OUTCOMES

✓ A 5 step plan to relax.

✓ Experience relaxation.

LESSON PLAN

➤ Ask the children to think of a time when they have watched their class baby get flustered, tetchy or fed up. What did their parents do?

➤ Ask the children to imagine and describe how the baby feels when they are gently held and snuggled by Mum or Dad or rocked and soothed.

For those classrooms not able to undertake the Circles for Learning Project, video clips or photographs can be used to support the discussion around the topic and stimulate thoughts and ideas from the children and young people.

Task

KS1: To experience a relaxation exercise.
KS2/3: To create a 5 step guide to relaxation.

KS1

1. Discuss the photos of people relaxing.

2. Talk about how their bodies feel – create metaphors:

   Calm like a pond

   Floppy like my teddy bear

   Still like a statue

   Tingly like a snowstorm ornament

3. Discuss a time when they feel calm and relaxed.

4. What is the opposite of calm and relaxed? Discuss how their body feels when they are energised and excited. Create metaphors for these feelings.

5. Draw a line to show how the two link on a spectrum.

6. Ask the children to stand on the line to show how they feel now. Put their name on a piece of paper to show where they are and leave it on the floor.

7. Pose the question – How do you get from energised and excited to calm and relaxed?

8. Explain to the children that you are going to do a relaxation exercise with them. To help them become even more relaxed.

9. Read the relaxation exercise 'Relax like a cat',

    http://www.moodcafe.co.uk/media/26930/Relaxleaflet.pdf

10. After the relaxation is completed, ask the children to go and stand on the relaxation line to show how they feel now. Is there a difference in how they were feeling before to now?

11. Use different relaxation strategies in the classroom on a daily basis to enable the children to learn how to relax and calm.

KS2/3
1. Ask the children to define relaxation.

2. Ask the children to think of a time when they felt relaxed. Can they describe that feeling?, e.g. my body felt calm like a still pond, my body felt floppy like a well-loved teddy bear.

3. Ask the children what the opposite of relaxed is – excited? energised? full of beans?

4. Draw a line to illustrate the spectrum and number it 1–10. Ask the children where they are now? Where were they at lunchtime?

5. Working in teams, ask the children to link the words and pictures and smells.

   • Relaxed

   • Exhilarated

   • Focused

6. Share the learning graph with the children and discuss where they do their best learning.

7. Ask them to share how they get from one stage to another – what strategies do they use.

   Excited to Focused

   Focused to Calm

   Calm to Focused

   Focused to Excited

8. Put the children in teams – the challenge is to create a 5 step guide to relaxation poster.

9. Discuss the success criteria together:

   ✓ The poster needs to contain 5 steps.

   ✓ There should be appropriate music playing throughout.

   ✓ It should help people to feel relaxed.

10. After completion get the class to assess each contribution against the success criteria.

11. Share a visualisation piece with the children:

    https://www.themindfulword.org/2012/guided-imagery-scripts-children-anxiety-stress/

RESOURCES

1. Relaxation exercise 'Relax like a cat':

   http://www.moodcafe.co.uk/media/26930/Relaxleaflet.pdf

2. Visualisation script:

   https://www.themindfulword.org/2012/guided-imagery-scripts-children-anxiety-stress/

3. Large flip chart

4. Pens for flip chart

5. Arousal Zone Graph

6. Sticky notes

7. Paper and pens

8. Coloured pens

9. Computer access

10. Selection of magazines and holiday brochures.

11. Lavender, lemon, mint, coffee, vanilla, basil scents or objects

IMPORTANT POINTS

• Steps to relaxation.

• Working together.

LEARNING LINKS

Speaking and listening, collaboration, information processing, questioning, observation, creativity, planning and organisation.

REFLECTION

Questions:

Positive comment from child:

Positive comment from adult:

LEARNING DIMENSIONS		SOCIAL & EMOTIONAL SKILLS	
Strategic awareness	▨	Emotional literacy	
Learning relationships	▨	Neuroscience	
Curiosity	▨	Self-regulation	▨
Creativity		Self-development	
Meaning making	▨		
Changing & learning			
Resilience			

Relaxed

Exhilarated

Focused

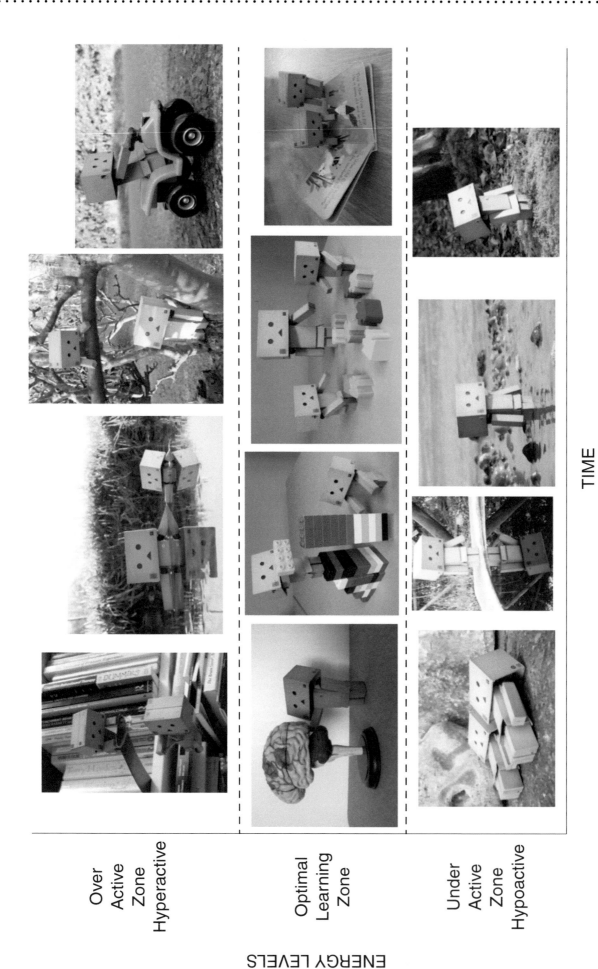

Over Active Zone Hyperactive

Optimal Learning Zone

Under Active Zone Hypoactive

ENERGY LEVELS

TIME

Thinking chains

SESSION OBJECTIVES

To explore the way we think.

To understand how one thought can lead to another.

To be aware that our brain likes patterns.

SESSION OUTCOMES

✓ To be able to play the Thinking Chain Game.

✓ To use thinking skills to remember things.

✓ To create a Mind Map to support learning.

LESSON PLAN

➢ Ask the children to remember/list all the things that their class baby has learnt to do.

➢ Share a memory of when they observed their class baby learn to do something.

➢ Discuss what their baby might have been thinking. How one thing led to another?

For those classrooms not able to undertake the Circles for Learning Project, video clips or photographs can be used to support the discussion around the topic and stimulate thoughts and ideas from the children and young people.

Task

KS1: To play the Thinking Chain Game.
KS2: Play Kim's Game and create a story to remember the objects.
KS3: To create a Mind Map to help learn about something.

Learning dimensions

KS1

1. Share with the children the Thinking Chain Game. Draw a chain on the board and ask a child to think of any word. Write the word in the chain. Then ask another child to say the word that the first one made them think of. Write that in the next link and so on.

2. Give the children the chains and ask them to play with a partner. How long can they make their chains?

3. When the chains have been completed, ask the children to share what they have found.

4. Discuss that our brains all make different links but that the groups are the same – demonstrate this by looking at the words chosen: CAT – DOG – both animals that we keep as pets; GREEN – RED – both colours; GREEN – TREES – a colour of something.

5. Ask the children how this knowledge can help us with our learning.

KS2

1. Ask the children if they have ever played Kim's Game. Explain what the game is.

2. Divide the class into 4 groups. Give each group a tray of 12 different objects . Tell them that they have 2 minutes to look at the objects and then you will cover them and as a team they have to try and remember as many as they can.

3. When their time is finished, cover the trays with a cloth and then ask them to write down as many things as they can remember.

4. Share how many things each group remembers.

5. Did anyone use a particular strategy?

6. Explain to the children that our brains like to find links or patterns and so remembering random objects is very hard for it. Tell the children that to help their brain remember they need to come up with a way to link the objects – has anyone any ideas? Link the objects in a story being as creative as they can.

7. Change the trays so that each group has a different tray. Give each group 2 minutes and then ask them to write down as many objects as they can remember. Have they increased the number of objects – did any group get all 12?

8. Ask the children how this piece of information might help them in their learning?

KS3

1. Play Kim's Game as above.

2. Ask the young people how this knowledge of how the brain works might help them in their learning? Link to Mind Maps and revision/note-taking.

3. Choose a subject that the class has some knowledge about – their mobile phone.

4. Create different categories and demonstrate these with branches of different colours – communication with others by text, WhatsApp, emails.

    Games

    Photographs

    Types of phones

    Contracts and providers

5. Give each group one of the headings to explore and draw out – like the branch of a tree. Each heading would be a different colour.

6. Share examples with the young people.

7. Ask each group to share what they have found and talk about how they can see this helping them with revision or note taking.

RESOURCES

1. Chains

2. Mind Maps

3. 4 trays with objects on for Kim's Game

IMPORTANT POINTS

Our mind makes links to help it remember and organise things.

We can use the need of our mind to make links to support us with revision or remembering things.

LEARNING LINKS

Working together, revision, neuroscience.

REFLECTION

Questions:

Positive comment from child:

Positive comment from adult:

LEARNING DIMENSIONS		SOCIAL & EMOTIONAL SKILLS	
Strategic awareness		Emotional literacy	
Learning relationships		Neuroscience	
Curiosity		Self-regulation	
Creativity		Self-development	
Meaning making			
Changing & learning			
Resilience			

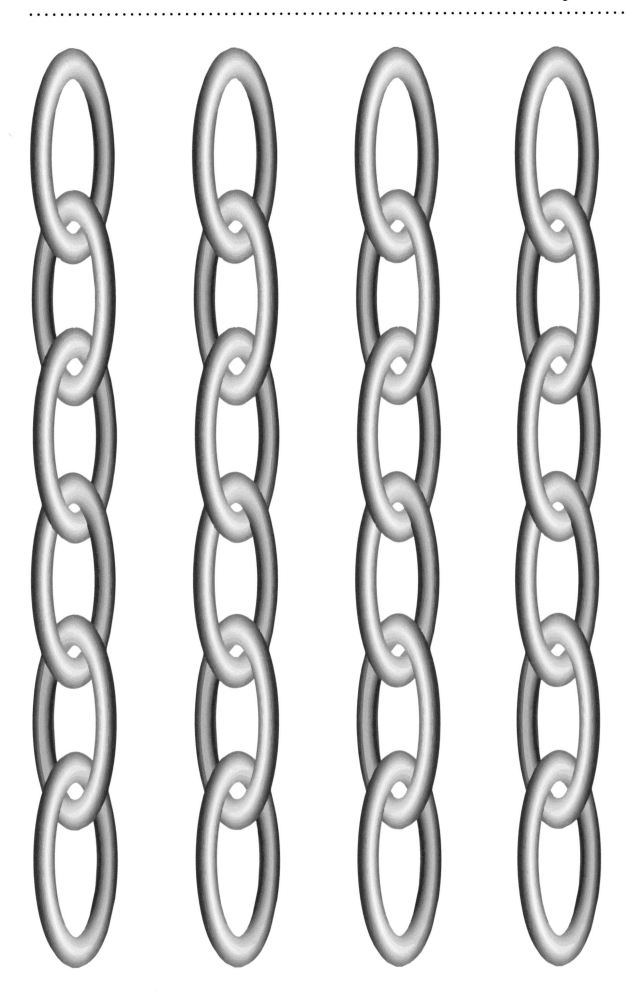

Everything that had to happen to make this

SESSION OBJECTIVES

To explore the way we think.

To understand how one thought can lead to another.

To be aware that our brain likes patterns.

SESSION OUTCOMES

✓ To be able list all the different things that had to happen to enable something to be in existence.

LESSON PLAN

➢ Ask the children to remember a toy that their class baby loved to play with.

➢ What was the toy made out of?

➢ Why did they like it?

For those classrooms not able to undertake the Circles for Learning Project, video clips or photographs can be used to support the discussion around the topic and stimulate thoughts and ideas from the children and young people.

Task

KS1: To share all the things that had to happen for an object to be in existence.
KS2/3: To share all the things that had to happen for an object to be in existence.

Learning dimensions

KS1

1. Share an object with the children – a flower – and ask them to share all the things that had to happen for the object to be there in front of them.

    Sunshine, rain, soil, seed, someone to help it grow, someone to pick it, someone to bring it in to them.

2. Give each group and object and ask them to think of all the things that had to happen for it to be in front of them.

3. Discuss how important the environment of our planet is and how much effort is put in to making things or growing them.

4. Discuss what they can do to support the environment at school:

    •   Pick up litter

    •   Recycle paper

    •   Turn off lights

    •   Be careful with water and turn off taps.

KS2/3

1. Share an object with the children – a book – and ask them to share all the things that had to happen for the object to be there in front of them: sunshine, rain, soil, seed, someone to cut the tree down, paper mill to make paper, chemicals to be added to the paper, someone to write the text, ink to print on the paper, packaging to send it to the shops, a shop to sell it, advertising to let people know about the book, someone to buy it.

2. Give each group and object and ask them to think of all the things that had to happen for it to be in front of them.

3. Write questions about their object that they may not know the answer to – How is ink made? What other things are added to paper to make it suitable to write on?

4. Share what they have discovered and the questions this has raised for them.

5. As a group find the answers to some of the questions that the activity raised for them.

6. What is one thing that they will take away from this activity?

7. For each person in the group they have worked with – What is one thing they have enjoyed about working with that person?

RESOURCES

1. A range of objects from natural materials – cork tile, woollen jumper, cup of milk, apple, flower, paper, silk, brick, piece of wood, china cup, glass.

IMPORTANT POINTS

Our mind makes links to help it remember and organise things.

We can use the need of our mind to make links to support us with revision or remembering things.

LEARNING LINKS

Working together, revision, neuroscience.

REFLECTION

Questions:

Positive comment from child:

Positive comment from adult:

LEARNING DIMENSIONS		SOCIAL & EMOTIONAL SKILLS	
Strategic awareness	�	Emotional literacy	
Learning relationships	▓	Neuroscience	
Curiosity	▓	Self-regulation	
Creativity		Self-development	▓
Meaning making	▓		
Changing & learning	▓		
Resilience			

Materials

Design

Transport

Safety
Checks

Reviews

Making

Buying and
Playing

Marketing

Strategic awareness

A sense of myself as someone who learns and changes over time

What is learning?

SESSION OBJECTIVES

To understand and explore what learning is.

SESSION OUTCOMES

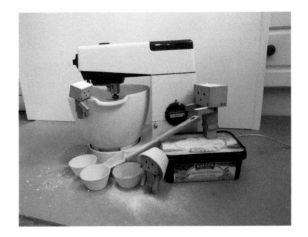

✓ To create a definition of what learning is and to be able to share examples of different types of learning that the children and young people have experienced.

LESSON PLAN

➤ Ask the children to describe a time when their watched their class baby learn to do something?

➤ Was that the only part of the learning – the end result? What had happened to enable them to get to that point?

For those classrooms not able to undertake the Circles for Learning Project, video clips or photographs can be used to support the discussion around the topic and stimulate thoughts and ideas from the children and young people.

Task

KS1: To make a poster.
KS2: To create a bookmark.
KS3: To make a video animation.

KS1

1. Ask the children to share a time when they had learnt to do something – in or out of school.

2. Help them break the learning into:

   • End result

   • Motivation

- Process or the learning journey

- Emotions they experienced

3. What skills did they need to achieve the end result?

4. Explore this question as a class.

5. Ask the children to create their own I Can Learn Poster.

KS2

1. Ask the children to share a time when they had learnt to do something – in or out of school.

2. Help them break the learning into:

   - End result

   - Motivation

   - Process or the learning journey

   - Emotions they experienced

3. What skills did they need to achieve the end result?

4. Explore this question as a class.

5. Ask the children to design and make a bookmark to remind them of the different stages when learning. The bookmark needs to contain:

   - A saying to help them keep motivated when the learning gets tough

   - 3 strategies to manage the emotions of learning

   - A sentence to help remind them that learning is a journey/process that happens over time and sometimes it can be easy and sometimes it can be hard

   - A sentence or saying to celebrate when they have achieved what they need to

   - 3 things they can do if they get stuck with their learning.

6. When they have completed they can share and talk about their bookmark with the other children in class.

7. Have they learnt other strategies that they didn't know about from someone else?

KS3

1. Ask the children to share a time when they had learnt to do something – in or out of school.

2. Help them break the learning into:

    •   End result

    •   Motivation

    •   Process or the learning journey

    •   Emotions they experienced

3. What skills did they need to achieve the end result?

4. Explore how our beliefs can impact on our learning

    •   I'm no good at maths

    •   I'm not very clever

    •   I can't do that

    •   This is too difficult for me. I am not as clever as …

5. Introduce the work of Carol Dweck on mindsets and the findings of neuroscientist that the brain is for ever learning and growing.

6. Ask the young people to create a PowerPoint or video animation to show the ups and downs of learning.

7. Share the work and discuss what they have found out or learnt.

RESOURCES

1. Tablet computer

2. Large paper

3. Pens

4. Pencils

5. Card

6.   I Can Learn Poster

7.   Laminator

IMPORTANT POINTS

• What we believe about ourselves a learner impact on how we learn and achieve.

• Learning is a process that happens over time.

• We all learn in different ways.

LEARNING LINKS

Speaking and listening, collaboration, information processing, questioning, observation, creativity, planning and organisation, teamwork.

REFLECTION

Questions:

Positive comment from child:

Positive comment from adult:

LEARNING DIMENSIONS		SOCIAL & EMOTIONAL SKILLS	
Strategic awareness	▓	Emotional literacy	▓
Learning relationships	▓	Neuroscience	
Curiosity		Self-regulation	
Creativity		Self-development	▓
Meaning making			
Changing & learning	▓		
Resilience	▓		

I Can Learn Poster

I learnt how to......

I wanted to learn how to do this because......

....

....

Skills I used when I was learning

I felt lots of emotions when I was learning. These are some of the emotions I felt.....

My learning strategies

SESSION OBJECTIVES

To identify my own ways of learning and to understand that I use different learning strategies for different things.

SESSION OUTCOMES

✓ My Learning Journey film strip.

✓ A list of learning strategies I have mastered.

LESSON PLAN

➢ Ask the children to remember a time when their class baby tried to complete a task – shape sorter, jigsaw, puzzle etc.

➢ What different strategies did they try?

➢ How did their mum help them?

➢ What emotions did they experience?

➢ How hard was it to watch them and not do it for them?

For those classrooms not able to undertake the Circles for Learning Project, video clips or photographs can be used to support the discussion around the topic and stimulate thoughts and ideas from the children and young people.

Task

KS1: To create a whole class If I Am Stuck Help Sheet.
KS2: To create a poster to support learning.
KS3: To create a PowerPoint presentation for a younger group on the ups and downs of learning and what to do.

Learning dimensions

KS1

1. Ask the children to think of a time when they became stuck with their learning. What did it feel like? What did they try? What was helpful?

2. As a group think about different things they can do when they get stuck.

3. Create a class Help Sheet to show the different things they can do when they get stuck or when their emotions take over and prevent them from learning.

4. Share what you have created with another class and explore what they think.

KS2

1. Ask the children to think of a time when they became stuck with their learning. What did it feel like? What did they try? What was helpful?

2. As a group think about different things they can do when they get stuck.

3. Remind the children of the work on Mindsets and Labels – how we think of ourselves and our abilities has a huge influence on what we do and what we achieve.

4. Divide the children into pairs and ask them to interview each other about something that they have achieved. Whilst one child talks the other writes down all the strategies they used to achieve what they did on sticky notes which they can then give to the person. Determination, creativity, persistence, observations, thinking, problems solving etc.

5. Together create a poster for the classroom to show different strategies that they can use when they get stuck.

6. The headings below could be used to scaffold the poster

    *   When I feel frustrated I can …

    *   When I don't know what to do I can …

    *   When I get confused I can …

    *   When I forget I can …

    *   When I get frightened of making a mistake I can …

    *   When I feel stupid I can …

    *   When I get overwhelmed I can …

    *   When I run out of energy I can …

7. When each pair has completed the poster have an exhibition and share with another class or group.

KS3

1. Ask the children to think of a time when they became stuck with their learning. What did it feel like? What did they try? What was helpful?

2. As a group think about different things they can do when they get stuck.

3. Remind the children of the work on Mindsets and Labels – how we think of ourselves and our abilities has a huge influence on what we do and what we achieve.

4. Divide the children into pairs and ask them to interview each other about something that they have achieved. Whilst one child talks the other writes down all the strategies they used to achieve what they did on sticky notes which they can then give to the person. Determination, creativity, persistence, observations, thinking, problems solving etc.

5. Divide the class into pairs or small groups.

6. Ask them to create an animation or a PowerPoint to share with a younger class on How to Manage the Ups and Downs of Learning.

7. Ask each group to present to the class and discuss what they all came up with.

RESOURCES

1. Help Sheet template

2. Sticky notes

3. Access to computers and PowerPoint or animation software

4. Large paper

5. Pens and colours

6. Planning sheet

IMPORTANT POINTS

- Understanding and celebrating the strategies we have already developed for learning.

- Experiencing that there are many learning strategies available to us that we can use for different learning.

LEARNING LINKS

Speaking and listening, collaboration, information processing, questioning, observation, creativity.

REFLECTION

Questions:

Positive comment from child:

Positive comment from adult:

LEARNING DIMENSIONS		SOCIAL & EMOTIONAL SKILLS	
Strategic awareness	▓	Emotional literacy	▓
Learning relationships	▓	Neuroscience	
Curiosity		Self-regulation	
Creativity		Self-development	▓
Meaning making	▓		
Changing & learning	▓		
Resilience	▓		

When I get stuck with my learning I can...

When I feel frustrated I can...

When I don't understand I can...

When I forget I can...

When I am confused I can...

When I don't know I can...

When I feel stupid I can...

149

My learning toolkit

SESSION OBJECTIVES

To identify the strategies I use when learning.

SESSION OUTCOMES

✓ My learning toolkit.

✓ A list of learning strategies I have mastered.

LESSON PLAN

➢ Ask the children to remember a time when they watched their class baby learn something.

➢ How did they achieve this? Was it something that they had been working on? Did their parent support them? How did they respond after they had achieved what they wanted?

For those classrooms not able to undertake the Circles for Learning Project, video clips or photographs can be used to support the discussion around the topic and stimulate thoughts and ideas from the children and young people.

Task

KS1: To create a learning toolkit.
KS2: To identify the strategies they have learnt that support their learning.
KS3: To identify the strategies they have already learnt to support their learning and to identify ones that they would still like to master.

KS1

1. Share with the children a piece of art work – a carving, painting or a sculpture. Discuss how many hours it has taken to produce and the array of tools that have been needed to create the piece of work.

2. Show them a toolkit.

3. Ask the children to come up with Learning Tools they have in their toolkit – ask them to draw and label them and add them to the toolkit.

4. Patience, persistence, resilience, stickability, creativity, problem solving.

5. Discuss with each other in pairs.

6. Share as a class – Which tool am I particularly pleased with? Which tool do I use most often? Which was the hardest tool to acquire? Which tools have I been given by my parents? Which tool would I like to have but have not got yet? Which tool would I like to give my partner to help them?

KS2

1. Share with the children a piece of art work – a carving, painting or a sculpture. Discuss how many hours it has taken to produce and the array of tools that have been needed to create the piece of work.

2. Show them a toolkit.

3. Ask the children to come up with Learning Tools they have in their toolkit. Work together to list the possibilities – creativity, ability to work with others, curiosity, persistence, resilience, problem solving, meaning making, mindset, bravery, courage, talking about how they learn, managing emotions, etc.

4. Ask the children to choose a tool and name it – discuss which tools they already have and give an example of when they have used it.

5. Share as a class – Which tool am I particularly pleased with? Which tool do I use most often? Which was the hardest tool to acquire? Which tools have I been given by my parents? Which tool would I like to have but have not got yet? Which tool would I like to give my partner to help them?

6. Add to their toolkit at different times when a new skill has been learnt. These can be specific – note taking, long division.

KS3

1. Share with the children a piece of art work – a carving, painting or a sculpture. Discuss how many hours it has taken to produce and the array of tools that have been needed to create the piece of work.

2. Show them a toolkit.

3. Discuss the different skills needed for learning in different areas.

4. As a class divide up and choose different areas of the curriculum and identify the Top 10 skills needed to be successful in the subject.

Art – creative, curious, good eye for shape and space, confidence, good eye for colour, brave, courageous, motivated, focused.

P.E. – full of energy, fit, healthy, motivated, persistent, work well in a team.

5. Share what they have identified. Are their skills that cross all areas?

6. Which skills do they feel they have already mastered, which skills do they hope to learn?

7. Introduce the area of motivation and link this to people who can do well. What enables a sportsperson to get up early every day and put in hours of training?

RESOURCES

1. Sculpture, art, carving

2. Toolkit

3. Blank toolkit

IMPORTANT POINTS

•   Understanding and celebrating the strategies we have already developed for learning.

•   Experiencing that there are many learning strategies available to us that we can use for different learning.

LEARNING LINKS

Speaking and listening, collaboration, information processing, questioning, observation, creativity.

LEARNING DIMENSIONS		SOCIAL & EMOTIONAL SKILLS	
Strategic awareness	▨	Emotional literacy	▨
Learning relationships	▨	Neuroscience	
Curiosity		Self-regulation	
Creativity		Self-development	▨
Meaning making	▨		
Changing & learning	▨		
Resilience	▨		

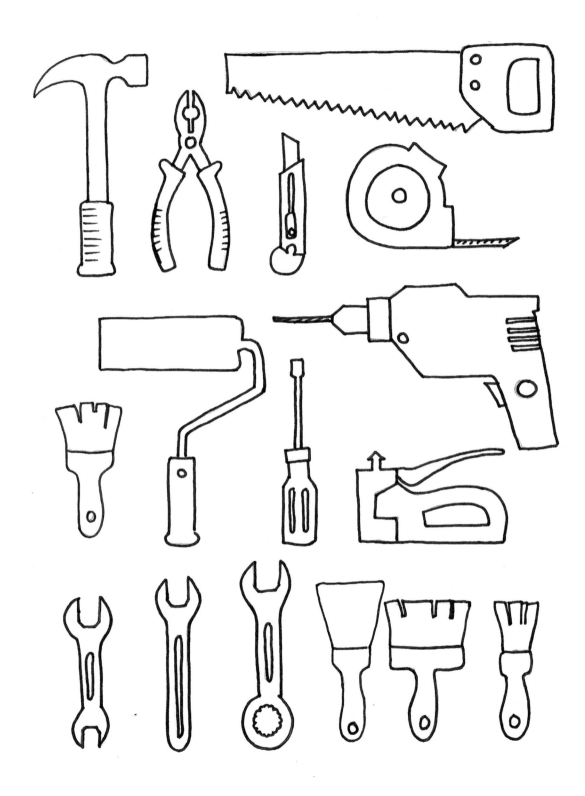

The emotions of learning

SESSION OBJECTIVES

To understand that when we learn we experience a range of emotions.

Emotions created by learning can be positive or negative to our ability to succeed.

SESSION OUTCOMES

✓ To be able to talk about the emotions we experience when learning.

✓ To be able to discuss strategies that we use to manage the emotions of learning.

✓ To create a postcard to show the emotion and the strategy they may use to manage that emotion.

LESSON PLAN

➢ Ask the children to share a time when they watched their class baby get cross because they couldn't do something.

➢ Ask the children to imagine how the baby felt and what clues they saw to support their idea.

➢ Discuss what the parent did to support the baby.

For those classrooms not able to undertake the Circles for Learning Project, video clips or photographs can be used to support the discussion around the topic and stimulate thoughts and ideas from the children and young people.

Task

KS1: To be able to talk about the emotions of learning and share how courageous they have been in a learning situation.

KS2/3: To be able to share some of the emotions that they feel when learning and some of the strategies that can be used to support them. To create a post card to share strategies.

KS1

1.   To read the children *Courage* by Bernard Waber.

2.   Discuss with the children why learning takes courage.

3.   Ask the children to work in pairs and draw and write when they have to have courage when learning:

     Courage is having a go when you are not sure.

     Courage is making a mistake and learning from it.

4.   Ask each pair to illustrate their statement and then create display for the class.

5.   Refer to this when you need the children to have courage in their learning.

KS2/3

1.   Ask the children to share all the different emotions that they experience when they are learning.

2.   Collect them in a list.

3.   Decide which are helpful and why and which are not helpful and why.

4.   Share with the children some art work that depicts different emotions – discuss the use of colour shape and form that the artist use.

5.   Ask the children to choose one negative or one positive emotion that they have felt and create a piece of art work to demonstrate what this feeling is like.

6.   By each picture ask the children to draw a cartoon person with the answer to how to manage the emotion, and a short note to say when they experienced this emotion.

7.   Create an exhibition to show the emotions of learning.

RESOURCES

1.   *Courage* by Bernard Waber

2.   Abstract art showing emotions

3.   Art work to show different emotions that might be felt by learners when attempting a task – fear, frustration, excitement, courage, stuckness

IMPORTANT POINTS

Learning is accompanied by emotions and sometimes these can be positive or negative.

Learning to manage the emotions of learning enables us to be a better learner.

LEARNING LINKS

Emotional literacy, self-awareness, creativity, teamwork, presentation, Literacy, problem solving.

REFLECTION

Questions:

Positive comment from child:

Positive comment from adult:

LEARNING DIMENSIONS		SOCIAL & EMOTIONAL SKILLS	
Strategic awareness		Emotional literacy	
Learning relationships		Neuroscience	
Curiosity		Self-regulation	
Creativity		Self-development	
Meaning making			
Changing & learning			
Resilience			

Performance and my Learning Zone

SESSION OBJECTIVES

To identify my peak performance and to be able to get myself into my Learning Zone.

SESSION OUTCOMES

✓ To be able to describe my performance curve in relation to my learning.

✓ To be able to describe a strategy I use to motivate myself into my Learning Zone and to calm myself when my learning is not going as well as planned.

LESSON PLAN

➢ Ask the children to remember a time when they watched their class baby behave in different ways – quiet, tired, excitable, full of energy, sleepy

➢ Ask them to describe what they say and then think about how the baby was feeling

➢ What did their parent do to help them in each case?

For those classrooms not able to undertake the Circles for Learning Project, video clips or photographs can be used to support the discussion around the topic and stimulate thoughts and ideas from the children and young people.

Task

KS1/2: To create a whole class graph to show concentration levels whilst working.

KS3: To plot their concentration levels throughout a task and describe how they motivated themselves to complete the task.

Learning dimensions

KS1/2

1. Introduce the words focus and concentration.

2. Discuss what they mean and when the children have experienced them.

3. Ask the children what the opposite of concentration is.

4. Undertake a learning task with the children explain that you will be stopping every 5 min to see what their concentration level is like. Use the line analogy with focused at one end and distracted at the other and numbers 1–10 on the line.

5. Explain the task they will be doing and take their concentration level.

6. Work on the task and take their concentration level every 5 minutes – add yours as their teacher and any other adults in the room.

7. When their concentration level drops to 5, stop the activity and do a short physical exercise – clapping game etc.

8. When you have finished, draw a graph to show the children how their concentration levels alter.

9. Discuss ways that they can keep themselves focused on a task.

KS3

1. Ask the children to define focus and concentration.

2. Ask what the opposite is.

3. Create a line to show both behaviours and number the line 1–10, 1 being distracted and 10 being focused.

4. Ask the children to plot where they are on the line throughout and activity.

5. Discuss what they found.

6. Discuss the learning journey that the children documented and identify when they were at their peak. Link this with playing football/netball and warming up and then cooling down.

7. Make links to how we feel (things that may happen before we get to school), emotions (how we feel about the subject), how our body feels (been out the night before or stayed up late, whether we had breakfast or have enough to drink). Link to the brain and what it needs to keep working – fuel in the car.

8. In pairs discuss how children get themselves motivated – what self-talk do they use?

9. What visualisation do they use for achieving their goals? Share the fact that David Beckham used visualisation techniques – imagining how he would take free kicks and seeing in his mind's eye the ball curl around and go in the net scoring a goal.

10. Share the different strategies that people use and choose the top 3 self-talk and the top 3 visualisation techniques.

11. Create bookmarks, posters, table top cards or postcards to help children remember the different strategies to motivate themselves and keep going when the going gets tough!

RESOURCES

1. Sticky notes

2. Performance curve

3. Card

4. Bookmarks

5. Postcards

IMPORTANT POINTS

- Understanding and celebrating the strategies we have already developed for learning.

- Experiencing that there are many learning strategies available to us that we can use for different learning.

LEARNING LINKS

Speaking and listening, collaboration, information processing, questioning, observation, creativity.

REFLECTION

Questions:

Positive comment from child:

Positive comment from adult:

Learning dimensions

LEARNING DIMENSIONS		SOCIAL & EMOTIONAL SKILLS	
Strategic awareness		Emotional literacy	
Learning relationships		Neuroscience	
Curiosity		Self-regulation	
Creativity		Self-development	
Meaning making			
Changing & learning			
Resilience			

Conscience alley

SESSION OBJECTIVES

To question and explore different viewpoints.

SESSION OUTCOMES

✓ A discussion exploring the pros and cons of a viewpoint/action.

✓ Discussion on potential consequences.

LESSON PLAN

➢ Ask the children to think of some of the questions they have asked the parent of their class baby.

➢ Discuss whether it is difficult or easy being a parent.

➢ What are some of the difficult decisions that a parent has to make?

For those classrooms not able to undertake the Circles for Learning Project, video clips or photographs can be used to support the discussion around the topic and stimulate thoughts and ideas from the children and young people.

Task

KS1: To discuss a point of view and say what they think and why.
KS2/3: To be able to have a debate on a statement and verbalise how they feel and why and explore the consequences of an action.

KS1

1. Give the class a statement – e.g. 'Children should all do 1 hour of P.E. every day'.

2. Ask the children to stand on one side of the class if they agree, the other side if they disagree and sit on the chairs at the front if they do not know.

163

3. Once the children are in place ask them to share why they believe they are on the side of the right answer.

4. After the Yes and No sides have shared their views ask the Don't Knows if they want to move.

5. Ask the other children if they wish to change.

6. Go through the procedure again and then count the numbers on each side.

KS2/3

1. On child is appointed to play a role, for example –the head teacher.

2. The child in role must make a decision on a given dilemma, for example, should children be set in ability groups across the school for Literacy and Maths?

3. The children must then discuss '**what ifs**'

4. Children take on a stance and line up on one side for and on the opposite side against, making an alleyway.

5. The child in role must walk down the alley/corridor that has been made, listening to the viewpoints as they go.

6. The child in role must then make a decision.

7. Discuss what influences our decision making – family, friends, media, television, etc.

8. Introduce the concept of bias.

9. This works just as well for other scenarios.

Judge – should a drink driver go to prison or serve the community?

Parent – should a child of 10 go to town with their friends?

Parent – should a parent be made to have their child vaccinated with the MMR jab?

RESOURCES

1. Large sheet of paper to write down questions and consequences.

IMPORTANT POINTS

• We all have different points of view about a range of things and these need to be respected.

• Our points of view are influenced by our friend's family and the media.

LEARNING LINKS

Speaking and listening, collaboration, information processing, questioning, observation, creativity, planning and organisation, teamwork.

REFLECTION

Questions:

Positive comment from child:

Positive comment from adult:

LEARNING DIMENSIONS		SOCIAL & EMOTIONAL SKILLS	
Strategic awareness		Emotional Literacy	
Learning Relationships		Neuroscience	
Curiosity		Self-Regulation	
Creativity		Self-Development	
Meaning making			
Changing & Learning			
Resilience			

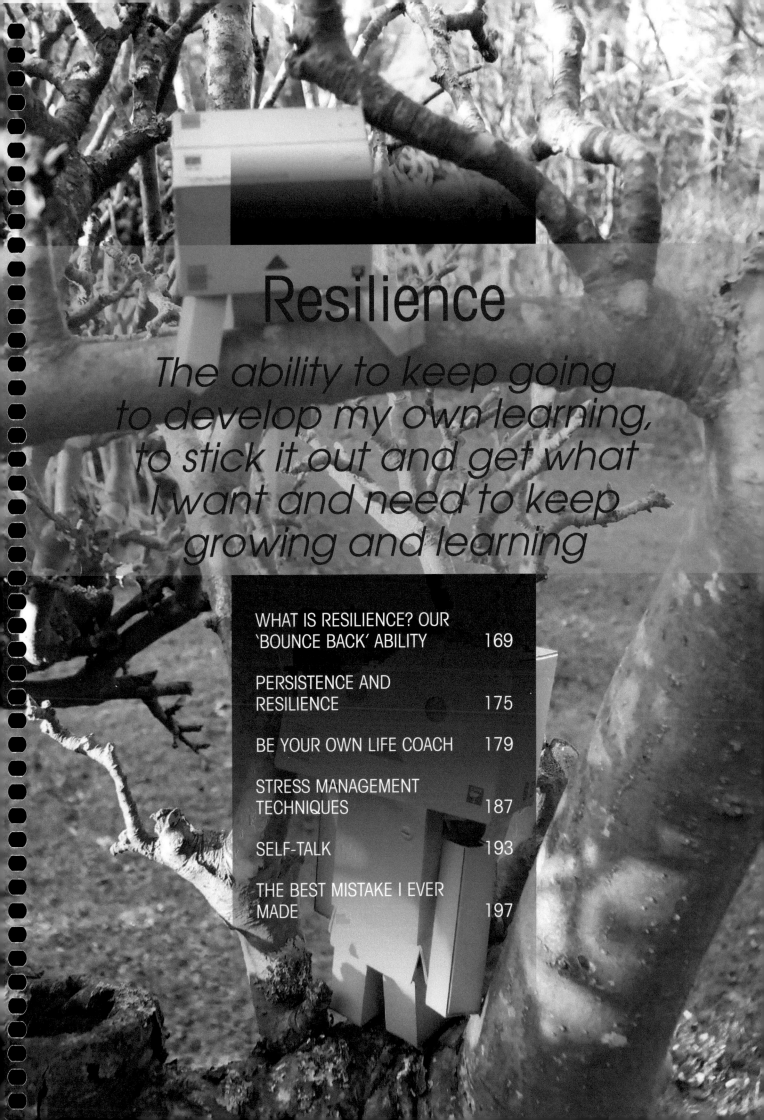

Resilience

The ability to keep going to develop my own learning, to stick it out and get what I want and need to keep growing and learning

What is resilience? Our `bounce back' ability

SESSION OBJECTIVES

To understand what resilience is and how we can strengthen it within ourselves.

SESSION OUTCOMES

✓ To create a poster/bookmark/animated video clip to remind us how important it is to develop our resilience and not give up.

LESSON PLAN

➢ Remind the children of a time when their class baby was finding things difficult. Discuss what they did, how they reacted and what the parent did, and how they responded.

➢ Remind them about how they felt when they saw the baby struggle and what they wanted to do – was this what the baby needed? How would they know?

➢ Share video clip.

For those classrooms not able to undertake the Circles for Learning Project, video clips or photographs can be used to support the discussion around the topic and stimulate thoughts and ideas from the children and young people.

Task

KS1: To be able to describe what resilience is and share a time when they were able to be resilient.

KS2/ KS3: To be able to define resilience and share strategies that they use to support themselves in managing difficult things.

KS1/KS2/KS3

1. Show the children a ball of modelling clay and tennis ball and ask what will happen if you drop them both?

2. Demonstrate and highlight how the modelling clay has got stuck and gone nowhere but the ball has bounced back ready to try again.

3. Explain that this is what resilience is – our 'bounce back' factor.

4. Ask the children/young people to think of a time when they found something really hard and gave up and walked away. How did they feel?

5. Ask them to think of a time when they found something really hard but kept going. – What kept them going? Was it: someone helping them, positive self-talk, the fact that there was a good reason?

6. How did they feel when they succeeded?

7. Discuss the different strategies that they have described and record them on the board. Ask them to choose which one they might try next time that they haven't tried before and why.

8. Record this as a class list – so you can check in on how they are doing in the future.

Poster

Discuss what a poster must share with people and identify the success criteria of a good poster.

- Eye-catching

- Colourful

- Catch-phrase

Ask the children to draw/use a photograph of themselves/find a photograph, that shows themselves or someone else being resilient.

Ask the children to find or create a catch-phrase to go with this and then create a poster to show what resilience is and to help people develop resilience.

Bookmark

Ask the children to think about why a bookmark could help them develop their resilience. Recap on the strategies they came up with in part 1.

Identify the success criteria for a good bookmark.

- Size

- Clear

- Catch-phrase

- Easy to understand

Ask the children to make a bookmark to remind them about resilience and strategies to use to help them bounce back.

Video/Animation

Ask the children to think about what makes a good animation.

Recap on the strategies to develop resilience that they identified in part 1.

Identify success criteria for a good animation about resilience.

- Clear

- Easily understood

- Short and to the point

When the children have completed their task ask them to share or create a mini exhibition where they can share their creation. Ask them to share how the ups and downs of creation and the process they had to go through.

Link how they respond to frustration and not being able to achieve something with the baby. Link how you as the teacher feel to the way the Mum responded. How you have to respond in 30 different ways!!

RESOURCES

1. Modelling clay

2. Ball

3. Pens for flip chart

4. Sticky notes

5. Paper and pens

6. Coloured pens

7. Card

8. Laminator

9. Sticky stars etc.

IMPORTANT POINTS

- That resilience can be strengthened and developed by developing different strategies.

- There are a variety of strategies that can help us be more resilient including self-talk, friends and beliefs about ourselves.

LEARNING LINKS

Speaking and listening, collaboration, information processing, questioning, observation, creativity, planning and organisation, teamwork.

REFLECTION

Questions:

Positive comment from child:

Positive comment from adult:

LEARNING DIMENSIONS		SOCIAL & EMOTIONAL SKILLS	
Strategic awareness	▓	Emotional literacy	▓
Learning relationships		Neuroscience	
Curiosity		Self-regulation	
Creativity		Self-development	▓
Meaning making	▓		
Changing & learning			
Resilience	▓		

Persistence and resilience

SESSION OBJECTIVES

To experience and practise what it means to be persistent and resilient.

To be able to keep going when things get difficult.

To pick yourself up and go again.

SESSION OUTCOMES

✓ Strategies for achieving our goals.

✓ Understand the importance of persistence and resilience in achieving our goals

LESSON PLAN

➤ Show the video clips of toddlers learning to stand and walk. Link with the observations of your class baby and how they have learnt to do things. Remind the children/young people about how difficult it has been at times.

➤ Ask them to identify what allows the toddler to continue.

For those classrooms not able to undertake the Circles for Learning Project, video clips or photographs can be used to support the discussion around the topic and stimulate thoughts and ideas from the children and young people.

Task

KS1: To draw a picture of a dog with their wrong hand and to be coached by a partner.
KS2/3: To draw a picture of a dog with their wrong hand and to be coached by a partner.

KS1/2

1. In pairs ask the children/young to decide who will be the coach and who will be the artist.

2. The artist is asked to draw a dog eating a bone with their wrong hand. The coach must give the artist advice and encouragement to improve their drawing and make them try 2 more times.

3. Ask the pairs to swap over. What had the coach learnt after being the artist? Did they do things differently?

4. Link with things the children/young people have learnt – reading, skateboarding, riding a bike. That they only learn by being persistent – keep going when it gets tough.

5. Get them to think of a time when they have done this.

6. Link with the work already done on being a good coach, your own best friend and self-talk.

7. In pairs write down the top 3 tips for positive coaching. Share these with the class and come up with the class top 10.

Introduce the concept WII4Me (What is in it for me)

KS3

1. In pairs ask the children/young to decide who will be the coach and who will be the artist.

2. The artist is asked to draw a house with a child and tree in the garden with their wrong hand. The coach must give the artist advice and encouragement to improve their drawing and make them try 2 more times.

3. Ask the pairs to swap over. What had the coach learnt after being the artist? Did they do things differently?

4. Discuss how it felt to be doing something that was difficult. How did having the coach help? What did they do?

5. How did motivation affect what you were doing? If you really want something is it easier to keep going?

6. What ways do you motivate yourself when undertaking homework?

RESOURCES

1. Paper

2. Pens

3. Blindfolds

4. Sticky notes

5. Paper and pens

6.   Toddlers learning to stand and walk videos:

   https://www.youtube.com/watch?v=vO6EQgzqvWg

   https://www.youtube.com/watch?v=G0oquuOq49I

IMPORTANT POINTS

*   Self-talk.

*   Belief in what we are doing.

*   Motivation strategies – giving yourself a reward, thinking about the end task and how good you will feel.

LEARNING LINKS

Speaking and listening, collaboration, information processing, questioning, observation, creativity, planning and organisation, teamwork.

REFLECTION

Questions:

Positive comment from child:

Positive comment from adult:

LEARNING DIMENSIONS		SOCIAL & EMOTIONAL SKILLS	
Strategic awareness	▓	Emotional literacy	▓
Learning relationships		Neuroscience	
Curiosity		Self-regulation	
Creativity		Self-development	▓
Meaning making	▓		
Changing & learning			
Resilience	▓		

Be your own life coach

SESSION OBJECTIVES

To develop the skills to be your own life coach.

SESSION OUTCOMES

✓ A list of positive comments.

✓ Understand the importance of feelings, thoughts and behaviour.

LESSON PLAN

➤ Remind the children of a time when they observed the parent of their class baby help the baby achieve something – putting a shape in the shape sorter, putting an object in a pot, putting the lid on a pot etc. Discuss how they did this. Their tone of voice, the words they used, their belief in the baby's ability.

➤ Remind them of how they felt when they observed the baby struggle.

➤ Remind them of the stages the baby when through before they succeeded in doing something.

For those classrooms not able to undertake the Circles for Learning Project, video clips or photographs can be used to support the discussion around the topic and stimulate thoughts and ideas from the children and young people.

Task

KS1: To write positive comments that could be said to yourself when you need support.
KS2: To write positive comments that could be said to yourself when you need support.
KS3: To write a selection of positive comments that a coach might use to help their mentee continue when learning gets difficult.

Learning dimensions

. . . .

KS1/KS2

1. Divide the class into groups. Ask each group to look at the coaching pictures and identify what skills the coach needs to have to help/support/develop/strengthen his team.

2. Imagine that the coaches' comments are like gold coins being put in the bank and that the players' negative comments/thoughts make the gold coins vanish. For the team/player to be successful the bank balance needs to be healthy.

3. Choose one of the pictures and then in groups write on the gold coins some of the comments that the coach might use to build his team/player up and make them feel positive about themselves and their abilities.

4. Share some of these comments with the other groups.

5. Choose the top 10 comments.

6. Remind the children and young people about being their own life coach. Help them explore the self-talk they use when doing a task or piece of work.

KS3

1. Divide the class into groups. Ask each group to look at the coaching pictures and identify what skills the coach needs to have to help/support/develop/strengthen his team.

2. Imagine that the coaches' comments are like gold coins being put in the bank and that the players negative comments/thoughts make the gold coins vanish. For the team/player to be successful the bank balance needs to be healthy.

3. Share the Thoughts, Feelings, Actions Triangle with the young people and discuss how our thoughts impact on what we can do and how we feel.

4. Remind the children and young people about being their own life coach. Help them explore the self-talk they use when doing a task or piece of work.

5. Ask them to write in the speech bubbles the things their personal coach might say to them when they are working.

6. Lay the comments around the class. Give the children 3 counters each and ask them to put a counter on their top 3 comments.

7. Discuss the results – why did they like the ones they had chosen, how would it make them feel if they could start to be their own self coach when learning?

. . . .

RESOURCES

1. Speech bubbles

2. Sticky notes

3. Photographs of coaches working with teams or individuals.

4. Thoughts, Feelings, Actions Triangle

5. Gold coins

6. Large piggy bank/pile of gold

IMPORTANT POINTS

-   We need to be our own best friend.

-   Self-talk is our internal coach.

LEARNING LINKS

Speaking and listening, collaboration, information processing, questioning, observation, creativity, planning and organisation, teamwork.

REFLECTION

Questions:

Positive comment from child:

Positive comment from adult:

Learning dimensions

LEARNING DIMENSIONS		SOCIAL & EMOTIONAL SKILLS	
Strategic awareness	▓	Emotional literacy	▓
Learning relationships		Neuroscience	
Curiosity		Self-regulation	
Creativity		Self-development	▓
Meaning making	▓		
Changing & learning			
Resilience	▓		

Learning dimensions

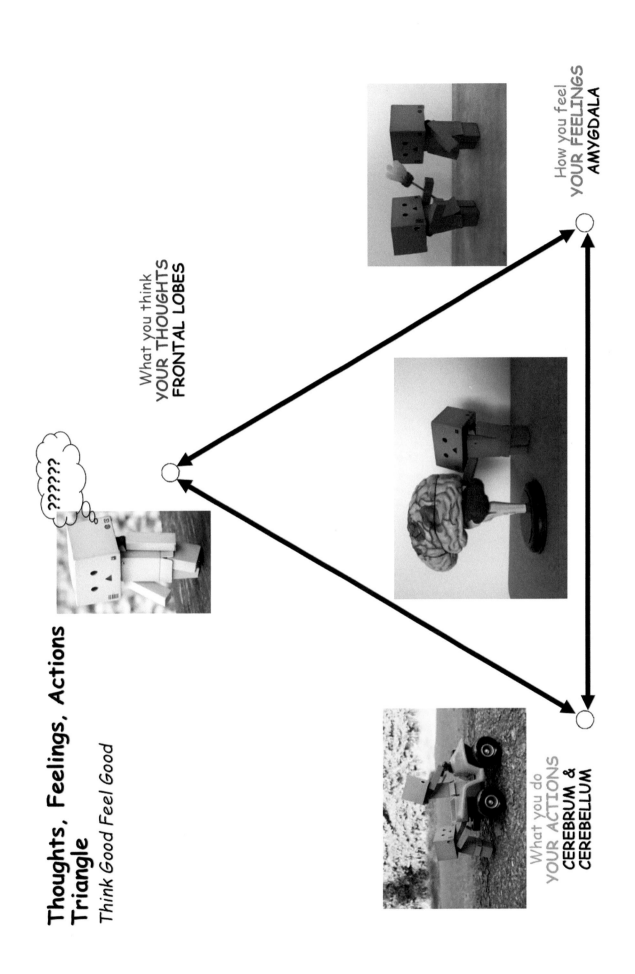

Thoughts, Feelings, Actions Triangle
Think Good Feel Good

What you think
YOUR THOUGHTS
FRONTAL LOBES

How you feel
YOUR FEELINGS
AMYGDALA

What you do
YOUR ACTIONS
CEREBRUM &
CEREBELLUM

?????

Stress management techniques

SESSION OBJECTIVES

To be able to identify stress in ourselves and manage this through developing a range of stress management techniques.

SESSION OUTCOMES

✓ Leaflet or poster of stress-busting strategies.

LESSON PLAN

➤ Remind the class of times when their class baby has been overwhelmed and has not been able to cope. Discuss what has happened to cause this and how they might feel.

➤ Identify strategies that helped the baby.

For those classrooms not able to undertake the Circles for Learning Project, video clips or photographs can be used to support the discussion around the topic and stimulate thoughts and ideas from the children and young people.

Task
KS2/KS3: To understand how stress make us feel.

Identify strategies to help us calm and relax.

Play Stress Room 101.

Create a Poster or leaflet to show a range of strategies to combat stress.

1. Discuss in pairs: What is stress? Is it good or bad? Do we need it? What purpose does it serve?

2. In pairs or small groups talk about a time when you were stressed, describe how it felt. List what happens to our mind and bodies when we become stressed.

3. Share the book *Silly Limbic* by Naomi Harvey (suitable for KS2 and some younger KS3 children).

4. Recap on the amygdala and its function. Share the hand brain.

5. Watch the Dan Siegel video:

   https://www.youtube.com/watch?v=f-m2YcdMdFw

6. Discuss what happens in the brain.

7. Discuss in pairs 3 things that you find stressful.

8. Introduce a relaxation exercise.

9. Play Stress Room 101. Each person can nominate a 'stressful' thing which they would like to be put into Room 101. At the end the class votes on which thing can go into room 101.

10. In pairs discuss 3 strategies you have for 'stress busting.'

11. Share these with the class.

12. Create a Stress Busting leaflet or poster to show a range of strategies to combat stress.

RESOURCES

1. Pictures showing people becoming stressed

2. Large box labelled Room 101

3. Paper and pens

4. Brain poster and the amygdala flight, fright, freeze responses

5. Relaxation exercise

6. YouTube clip of the hand brain analogy:

   https://www.youtube.com/watch?v=f-m2YcdMdFw

7. *Silly Limbic* by Naomi Harvey

IMPORTANT POINTS

- Stress is a natural reaction when we feel under threat.

- We can manage our stress in a variety of ways.

- Relaxation, focusing on breathing, distraction, creative activities may all help us manage stress.

LEARNING LINKS

Thoughts, feelings, actions, self-talk, own best friend, relaxation.

REFLECTION

Questions:

Positive comment from child:

Positive comment from adult:

LEARNING DIMENSIONS		SOCIAL & EMOTIONAL SKILLS	
Strategic awareness	▩	Emotional literacy	▩
Learning relationships		Neuroscience	▩
Curiosity		Self-regulation	
Creativity		Self-development	▩
Meaning making	▩		
Changing & learning			
Resilience	▩		

THE STRESS RESPONSE: WHAT HAPPENS INSIDE OUR BODY?

Stress is both a biological and psychological response that the body experiences when it believes it is under a threat which we believe we do not have the skills or abilities to deal with.

A stressor is the stimulus (or threat) that causes stress response within the body e.g. exam, moving school, loss of a friend, separation from a loved one.

Sudden and severe stress causes these effects in the body:

◆ Increased heart rate

◆ Increase in breathing, which often becomes shallow and fast (lungs dilate)

◆ Decrease in digestive activity, which is often why we feel butterflies in our tummy (don't feel hungry)

◆ Liver releases glucose for energy – so we become fidgety and can't sit still

When something happens our body looks at the information it has and decides whether or not it is stressful. This decision is made based on sensory information (i.e. the things we see and hear in the situation) and also on our memories (i.e. what happened the last time we were in a similar situation).

If the brain decides that the situation is stressful, the hypothalamus (at the base of the brain) is activated.

The hypothalamus in the brain is in charge of the stress response. When a stress response is triggered, it sends signals to two other structures: the **pituitary gland**, and the **adrenal medulla**.

These short term responses are produced by The Fight or Flight Response via the Sympathomedullary Pathway (SAM). Long term stress is regulated by the Hypothalamic Pituitary-Adrenal (HPA) system.

The Hypothalamic Pituitary–Adrenal (HPA) System

1. The Hypothalamic Pituitary Axis (HPA) is activated by the stressor

2. The hypothalamus stimulates the pituitary gland

3. The pituitary gland secretes adrenocorticotropic hormone (ACTH)

4. ACTH stimulates the adrenal glands to produce the hormone corticosteroid

5. Cortisol enables the body to keep a steady supply of blood sugar

A steady supply of blood sugar helps the body to cope with stress that goes on for a long time and then helps the body to return to normal.

The adrenal glands releases stress hormones called cortisol. The hormone cortisol has a number of functions it releasing stored glucose from the liver (for energy) and controls any swelling that may have been created. To enable the body to focus on reducing swelling and making sure the body has enough sugar the immune system stops working at its full capacity.

Sympathomedullary Pathway (SAM)

Once a stressor is identified the hypothalamus also activates the adrenal medulla. The adrenal medulla is part of the autonomic nervous system (ANS).

The ANS is the part the nervous system that acts as a control system, maintaining homeostasis in the body. Homeostasis is how the body keeps conditions inside it the same. It is the maintenance of a constant internal environment.

Two examples of things that the body keeps the same are:

body temperature at 37°C
the amount of water inside our body

These activities are generally performed without conscious control.

The adrenal medulla secretes the hormone adrenaline. This hormone gets the body ready for a fight or flight response. Physiological reaction includes increased heart rate, dry mouth, quickening of breathing.

Adrenaline causes the sympathetic nervous system to become aroused and this reduces the activity in the parasympathetic nervous system.

Adrenaline creates changes in the body such as decreases (in digestion) and increases (sweating, increased pulse and blood pressure).

Once the 'threat' is over the parasympathetic branch takes control and brings the body back into a balanced state.

No ill effects are experienced from the short-term response to stress and it further has survival value in an evolutionary context.

Self-talk

SESSION OBJECTIVES

To identify the self-talk that we use.

To turn the negative self-talk into positive self-talk.

SESSION OUTCOMES

✓ To be able to create positive self-talk when we need to undertake a difficult task or cope with something hard.

LESSON PLAN

➢ Ask the children to think about what they have learnt about being a parent from the class baby parent?

➢ Was it as easy as people had thought it would be?

➢ How do the parents cope with self-doubt?

For those classrooms not able to undertake the Circles for Learning Project, video clips or photographs can be used to support the discussion around the topic and stimulate thoughts and ideas from the children and young people.

Task

KS1 To identify what messages we give ourselves when we are undertaking a difficult task.
KS2/3 To identify the self-talk we use when we are doing something difficult.
    To change the negative self-talk into something positive.

KS1/2

1. Give the children a puzzle – matchsticks puzzles are good.

2. Ask them to work on the puzzle on their own.

3. Read the children the story *The Most Magnificent Thing* by Ashley Spires.

4. Ask the children to give you examples of what the little girl is saying to herself as you read through the story. Focus on the negative self-talk and how that is making her feel.

5. If she was their friend what would they be saying to her?

6. Help them think about changing the negative phrases to positive ones.

7. Ask them to draw a picture of themselves doing the puzzle and put red negative self-talk on one side and green positive self-talk on the other.

8. Ask them how they could change the red to the green.

KS3

1. Give the children a puzzle – matchstick puzzles are good.

2. Ask them to work at this on their own for a few minutes.

3. Share the video clip of a 600 m race:

    https://www.youtube.com/watch?v=xjejTQdK5OI

    Think about the self-talk that is taking place from the athletes.

4. Ask the young people to listen to their own self-talk as they complete the puzzle.

5. Share the book *I Can't Do This* by K. J. Walton.

6. Ask the children to share some of the self-talk and then change the message.

    I can't – cut off the 't' and you get can or I can't do this YET

    I'm no good at this – I can learn how to improve

    I'm useless at this – I can improve if I practise

    Set the challenge – one side to come up with the negative – red – and the other to change it – green.

RESOURCES

1. Sticky notes

2. *The Most Magnificent Thing* by Ashley Spires

3. *I Can't Do This* by K.J. Walton

4. Plain paper and pens

5. Red and green felt tip pens

6. Paper

7. Video clip:

    https://www.youtube.com/watch?v=xjejTQdK5OI (accessed 1 January 2019)

IMPORTANT POINTS

We can change our self-talk from negative to positive.

If we treat ourselves as we would do our friends then we would be much kinder and our self-talk would be more positive.

LEARNING LINKS

Speaking and listening, collaboration, information processing, questioning, observation, creativity, planning and organisation, teamwork.

REFLECTION

Questions:

Positive comment from child:

Positive comment from adult:

LEARNING DIMENSIONS		SOCIAL & EMOTIONAL SKILLS	
Strategic awareness	▓	Emotional literacy	▓
Learning relationships		Neuroscience	
Curiosity		Self-regulation	
Creativity		Self-development	▓
Meaning making	▓		
Changing & learning			
Resilience	▓		

The best mistake I ever made!

SESSION OBJECTIVES

To enable children to explore the benefits of mistakes.

To enable children to celebrate mistakes and identify what they gained from making them.

SESSION OUTCOMES

✓ To understand the learning opportunities that a mistake can give.

LESSON PLAN

➤ Ask the children to think about their class baby and identify a time when they got something wrong. Ask the children to think about what that enable the baby/toddler to then go onto doing.

➤ Ask the children what they think it must be like to be a parent – How do you know what to do? Explore whether they think parents make mistakes.

For those classrooms not able to undertake the Circles for Learning Project, video clips or photographs can be used to support the discussion around the topic and stimulate thoughts and ideas from the children and young people.

Task

KS1 To draw a picture or share 'My Best Mistake Ever' and explain what they learnt from it.
KS2/3 To create a gallery of mistakes showing mistakes that had been made and what the children/young people/adults got out of them.

KS1/2

1. Show the children a picture of a bottle of medicine. Share the story of how penicillin was found. Fleming left the top off the Petri dish and discovered it for the first time.

2. Share a picture of the Leaning Tower of Pisa. Talk about how the architect and builder must have felt. Explore with the children what they might have learnt and taken into the future with them.

3. Ask the children to draw a picture of their best ever mistake. Ask them to share with each other and talk about what they learnt.

4. Ask them to draw how they feel when they make a mistake on one side of the paper and then to create a speech bubble to show what their Inner Coach is saying to help them understand it is OK and really important to their learning on the other.

KS2/3

1. Show the children the YouTube clip about how penicillin came about.

2. Share a picture of the Leaning Tower of Pisa. Talk about how the architect and builder must have felt. Explore with the children what they might have learnt and taken into the future with them.

3. Put the children into pairs. Ask them to share a mistake they have made. How did they feel? What did they do to manage this feeling? What was the self-talk that they used?

4. Share these together and compile a list of feelings experienced when making mistakes. Compile a list of ways of managing these feelings.

5. What would their Internal Coach say about the mistake?

6. Create a board for 'Best Mistake of the Week'. Ask visiting teachers to contribute. Ask teachers to send in their best mistake and what they took from them and play room 101.

RESOURCES

1. The story of penicillin:

   https://www.youtube.com/watch?v=OZWjzcsTd5M

2. The story of the Leaning Tower of Pisa

3. Plain paper and pens

4. Photographs of mistakes: Leaning Tower of Pisa, penicillin, Christopher Columbus, the Titanic

IMPORTANT POINTS

Mistakes are important in the learning process. Learning how to manage and cope with them is important in developing resilience.

LEARNING LINKS

Speaking and listening, collaboration, information processing, questioning, observation, creativity, planning and organisation, teamwork.

REFLECTION

Questions:

Positive comment from child:

Positive comment from adult:

LEARNING DIMENSIONS		SOCIAL & EMOTIONAL SKILLS	
Strategic awareness		Emotional literacy	�
Learning relationships		Neuroscience	
Curiosity		Self-regulation	
Creativity		Self-development	▨
Meaning making	▨		
Changing & learning	▨		
Resilience	▨		

Creativity

Risk taking, playfulness, imagination and intuition

My Little Book of Ideas

SESSION OBJECTIVES:

To create a Little Book of Ideas.

SESSION OUTCOMES

✓ To be able to discuss the meaning of the word creativity.

✓ To have created a Little Book of Ideas or My Little Book of Inspiration.

✓ To be able to identify a range of pictures quotes, videos and music that inspire.

✓ To create a Classroom Inspiration board.

LESSON PLAN

➢ Ask the children to describe a time when they watched their class baby use their imagination.

For those classrooms not able to undertake the Circles for Learning Project, video clips or photographs can be used to support the discussion around the topic and stimulate thoughts and ideas from the children and young people.

Task

KS1: To create a Little Book of Ideas.
KS2: To be able to discuss creativity and the things that inspire them to be creative.

To be able to create a Tips for … book.

KS1

1. Read the book *What Do You Do with an Idea?*, by Kobi Yamada.

2. Ask the children to draw 'A Little Idea'.

3. Give each of the children an art book or a folder and ask them to start collecting ideas that they have or pictures that inspire them.

4. Share what they have and why it is important or inspirational to them.

5. Create a class Inspirations Noticeboard where anybody can pin up or share things that they are inspired by, great ideas or great thoughts they have had.

KS2/3

1. Discuss what the children understand by creativity. When were they last creative? How did it feel? Do they enjoy being creative or is it scary?

2. Collect or research creative phrases or sayings.

3. Bring to the group their favourite and explain why they like it.

4. Share the story *Ishi* by Akiko Yabuki with the children.

5. Ask them to create a series of pictures and phrases that link to a theme of their choice – Tips on how to be a great friend, Tips on how to succeed at school, Tips on how to revise, Tips on how to manage stress, Tips on staying safe on social media etc.

6. Share the pocket books when they have completed them.

RESOURCES

1. *Ishi* by Akiko Yabuki

2. Paper

3. Card

4. Stapler

5. Magazines and books of inspirational quotes

6. *What Do You Do with an Idea?* by Kobi Yamada

7. Folders and art books

8. Phones/cameras

9. Access to computers

IMPORTANT POINTS

Creativity is about playing with ideas.

You have to be brave to play and try out ideas.

LEARNING LINKS

Working together, emotional literacy, creativity, problem solving, self-awareness.

REFLECTION

Questions:

Positive comment from child:

Positive comment from adult:

LEARNING DIMENSIONS		SOCIAL & EMOTIONAL SKILLS	
Strategic awareness		Emotional literacy	▓
Learning relationships	▓	Neuroscience	
Curiosity		Self-regulation	
Creativity	▓	Self-development	▓
Meaning making			
Changing & learning	▓		
Resilience			

Thinking up a storm

SESSION OBJECTIVES

To explore some creativity tasks.

SESSION OUTCOMES

✓ To explore and play with some creativity activities and games.

✓ To be able to describe the process of being creative.

LESSON PLAN

➢ Ask the children to remember a time when their class baby had shown creative behaviour.

➢ Discuss what creativity is and examples of when they have been creative.

For those classrooms not able to undertake the Circles for Learning Project, video clips or photographs can be used to support the discussion around the topic and stimulate thoughts and ideas from the children and young people.

Task

KS1: To experiment with being creative.
KS2/KS3: To be able to describe what creativity is and give examples of when they have been creative.

KS1

1. Ask the children about the last time they used their creative muscle. Talk about what they did and why and how it felt.

2. What is the opposite of creative? Unimaginative?

3. Ask the children to place themselves on the creative line – creative one end and unimaginative or uncreative the other end.

4.   Remind them that how they think will influence what they can do!! What is their evidence for standing in this place?

5.   Teach the children how to play the squiggle game. Ask the children to get into pairs. Each person has a piece of paper. Each person needs to choose a colour felt tip. With their felt tip they draw a squiggle. They swap the paper over so that their partner gets their squiggle and vice versa. Their partner then has to turn their squiggle into a picture.

6.   Share what they have done with each other.

KS2/3

1.   Working in pairs, ask the children to define creativity and give an example of when they last used their creativity muscles.

     Creativity is intelligence having fun!

2.   What is the opposite of creative? Unimaginative?

3.   Ask the children to place themselves on the creative line – creative one end and unimaginative or uncreative the other end.

4.   Remind them that how they think will influence what they can do!! What is their evidence for standing in this place?

5.   Divide the children into groups and ask them to come up with as many uses of for a paperclip as they can in 5 minutes – they can be as creative as they like!

6.   Give the children the large circles sheet/small circles sheet or the complete the picture sheet. With the circles sheet ask them to create as many pictures as they can.

7.   Share what they have done.

8.   What does it feel like to be creative – who enjoys it, who dislikes it and why?

RESOURCES

1.   Finish the drawing

2.   Small circles creative sheet

3.   Large circles creative sheet

4.   Pens, pencils and felt tips

IMPORTANT POINTS

Creativity is exploring and playing with things and seeing what happens.

LEARNING LINKS

Working together, creativity, playing, sharing ideas, problem solving.

REFLECTION

Questions:

Positive comment from child:

Positive comment from adult:

LEARNING DIMENSIONS		SOCIAL & EMOTIONAL SKILLS	
Strategic awareness		Emotional literacy	
Learning relationships		Neuroscience	
Curiosity	▓	Self-regulation	
Creativity	▓	Self-development	▓
Meaning making			
Changing & learning	▓		
Resilience			

Learning dimensions

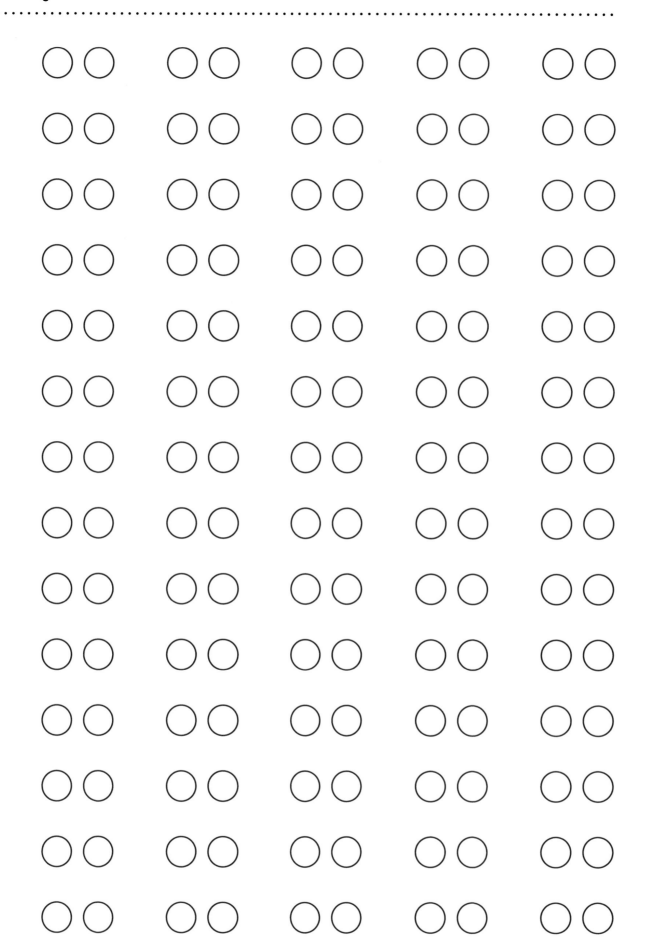

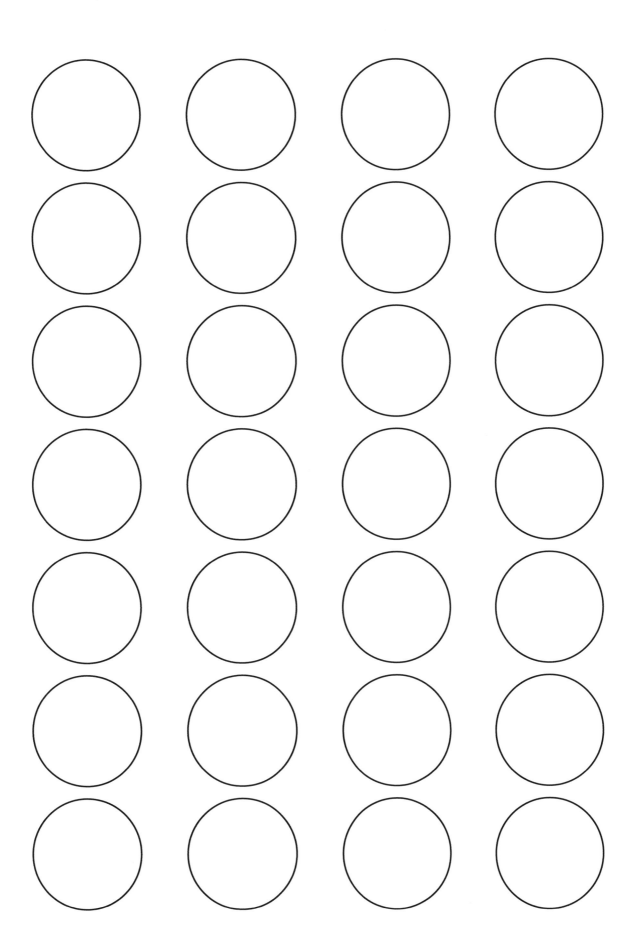

CAN YOU TURN THESE LINES INTO A PICTURE?

Ready steady make a game

SESSION OBJECTIVES

To work with a group of other children and to create a game.

SESSION OUTCOMES

✓ To create, plan and make a game.

✓ To review and give feedback to others about their game.

LESSON PLAN

➢ Ask the children to remember a time when their class baby had brought in a toy.

➢ What was the purpose of the toy, how was it used?

➢ How did their class baby respond to the toy?

For those classrooms not able to undertake the Circles for Learning Project, video clips or photographs can be used to support the discussion around the topic and stimulate thoughts and ideas from the children and young people.

Task

KS1: To create a game to play with others.
KS2/KS3: To work in a group and design plan and create a game to play with other young
     people.
          To give feedback to other groups about their game.

KS1

1. Ask the children to share with you as many games as they can think of and give them a FUN factor level out of 10.

2. List the games in categories – Board Games, Outside Games, Card Games, Small World Toy Games.

3. Set the children the challenge of making a board game of their own in groups/pairs

4. Share the board game templates and ask the children to choose which one they would like to work with.

5. Ask the children to discuss in their groups or pairs:

    a.   What is the aim of the game? – to get to the end, collect things, capture things, rescue things etc.

6. What are the difficulties that have to be managed? – in snakes and ladders this is the ladders and snakes but this could be danger squares, problem squares, monster squares etc.

7. How many can play the game?

8. Ask them to draw a rough draft of the game so that they can share with others.

9. Present their game to the group.

10. Ask the group to give four comments as feedback:

11. I like…

12. It would be good if you could…

13. I think you should think about … because…

14. I am really impressed by…

15. Ask the children to make a plan for how they will make their game – share this with the group – and receive feedback.

16. Make the game.

17. Have a fun games afternoon playing all the games.

KS2/3

1. Ask the children to share with you as many games as they can think of and give them a FUN factor level out of 10.

2. List the games in categories – Board Games, Outside Games, Card Games, Small World Toy Games.

3. Set the children the challenge of making a board game of their own in groups/pairs.

4. Ask the children to create a game and a draft of what that would look like and share that with the class.

5. After the presentations of the games as one group to give feedback to another group. Using the headings:

   ✓ I like…

   ✓ It would be good if you could…

   ✓ I think you should think about … because…

   ✓ I am really impressed by…

6. Create a planning sheet to document how the game will be played and who will do what – remind the children of the fact that for good teamwork:

   • People work on things they are comfortable with

   • It is best to use people skills in the creation of a project

   • All of the team needs to give creative feedback to each other

7. Make the games and then try them out – feed back to the group any alterations that were made to make the game better.

8. Complete the game and then have an afternoon of fun to try them all out.

9. Each group to leave a review of the game on the table and give it a star rating.

RESOURCES

1. Card

2. Paper

3. Pens

4. Blank playing cards

5. Dice

6. Counters

7. Glue sticks

8. Rulers

IMPORTANT POINTS

Good planning means that all the group are involved and that their skills are utilised in the creation of the end product.

Reviewing a project is an important way of ensuring that difficulties are sorted.

LEARNING LINKS

Teamwork, problem solving, planning, reviewing, collaboration, constructive feedback.

REFLECTION

Questions:

Positive comment from child:

Positive comment from adult:

LEARNING DIMENSIONS		SOCIAL & EMOTIONAL SKILLS	
Strategic awareness		Emotional literacy	
Learning relationships	░	Neuroscience	
Curiosity		Self-regulation	
Creativity	░	Self-development	░
Meaning making			
Changing & learning	░		
Resilience			

100	99	98	97	96	95	94	93	92	91
81	82	83	84	85	86	87	88	89	90
80	79	78	77	76	75	74	73	72	71
61	62	63	64	65	66	67	68	69	70
60	59	58	57	56	55	54	53	52	51
41	42	43	44	45	46	47	48	49	50
40	39	38	37	36	35	34	33	32	31
21	22	23	24	25	26	27	28	29	30
20	19	18	17	16	15	14	13	12	11
1	2	3	4	5	6	7	8	9	10

Learning dimensions

START

FINISH

Good luck bad luck

SESSION OBJECTIVES

To understand that how we think about a situation impacts on how we behave and how we feel.

By reframing – or thinking about situations in a different way – we can help ourselves feel and manage difficulties in a better way.

SESSION OUTCOMES

✓ To reframe what could be difficult situations.

✓ To challenge each other to think of ways out of situations with the Good Luck Bad Luck game.

LESSON PLAN

➤ Ask the children to remember when their baby created a mess/broke something or caused a problem for their parent.

➤ How did their class parent respond?

For those classrooms not able to undertake the Circles for Learning Project, video clips or photographs can be used to support the discussion around the topic and stimulate thoughts and ideas from the children and young people.

Task

KS1 : To play the game Good Luck Bad Luck.
KS2/KS3: To reframe a situation into a more positive way of thinking about it.

KS1

1. Read the story *Good News Bad News* By Jeff Mack.

2. Discuss how the different ways of thinking makes the animals feel.

3. Play the Good Luck Bad Luck game with the children.

KS2/3

1. KS2 – Read the book *Mr Sherman's Cloud* by David Habben.

2. Discuss the fact that how we think about the situation affects how we feel about it and then how we behave.

3. Remind the children of the Thoughts, Feelings, Actions Triangle.

4. Introduce the words Optimistic and Pessimistic and discuss how people may develop these traits – their experiences and the way they think about them. They have a thought and then the brain looks for evidence to support that thought.

    Optimism – Hopefulness and confidence about something.

    Pessimistic – Tending to see the worst aspects of something or believing the worst may happen.

5. Have they ever had a friend who no matter what they say is not able to change what they believe?

6. Ask the children to draw a cartoon character for both Optimism and Pessimism.

7. Share a range of photos and challenge the children to a competition.

8. Create the Optimisms and the Pessimisms and an audience who can vote.

9. Share a picture and ask each for their 'thoughts'. Whoever has the most imaginative thought is the winner of the point. E.g. Box person in the mud – Oh now I'm going to drown in mud OR Well this gives me the perfect opportunity to test out how well my washing powder works.

RESOURCES

1. *Good News Bad News* by Jeff Mack

2. *Mr Sherman's Cloud* by David Habben

3. Thinking Circle diagram

4. A selection of photographs showing potential disasters

IMPORTANT POINTS

How we think impacts on how we feel and how we behave.

If we can develop the skills of optimistic thinking and reframing situations then we can have an impact on how we feel.

LEARNING LINKS

Working together, emotional literacy, speaking and listening, creativity, problem solving, self-awareness, self-talk.

REFLECTION

Questions:

Positive comment from child:

Positive comment from adult:

LEARNING DIMENSIONS		SOCIAL & EMOTIONAL SKILLS	
Strategic awareness		Emotional literacy	▓
Learning relationships		Neuroscience	
Curiosity		Self-regulation	
Creativity	▓	Self-development	▓
Meaning making			
Changing & learning	▓		
Resilience	▓		

Learning dimensions

Thinking Circle

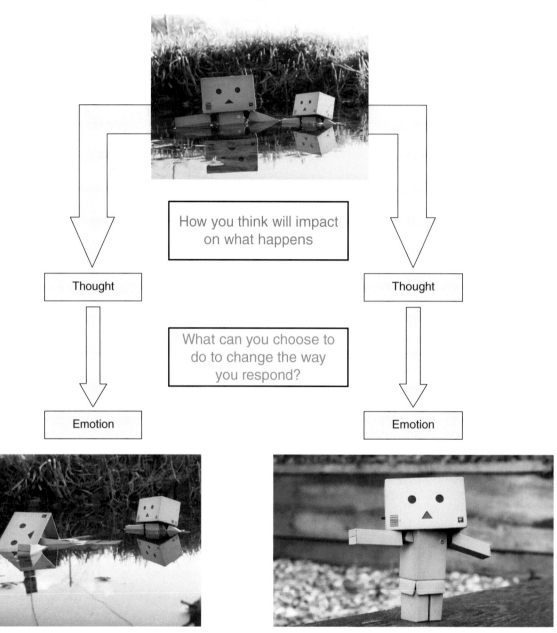

How you think will impact on what happens

Thought

Thought

What can you choose to do to change the way you respond?

Emotion

Emotion

Chapter 3
Problem solving

Problem solving 1

SESSION OBJECTIVES

To explore problem solving strategies.

To work within a group to solve a problem.

To understand the importance of adaptability
   when trying to solve problems.

SESSION OUTCOMES

✓   To build a model shelter as a team with an assortment of bits and pieces.

✓   To explore the problem solving method.

LESSON PLAN

➢   Ask the children to remember a time when their class baby had to solve a problem.

➢   What did they do? How did their parent support them?

For those classrooms not able to undertake the Circles for Learning Project, video clips or photographs can be used to support the discussion around the topic and stimulate thoughts and ideas from the children and young people.

Task

KS1: Working in pairs build a model shelter from the kit provided.
KS2/3: Working in small groups or pairs create a model shelter from the kit provided that can withstand the force of Arctic winds – a fan!

KS1

1.   Share the story with the children. They are lost in the Arctic and need to build a shelter. One of them has snow blindness and so is not able to see; the other has frostbite on their hands so cannot touch anything. Together they have to build a model shelter from the kit provided.

2.   Tell the children that they have 30 minutes to build their shelter.

3. Blindfold the child who is going to have snow blindness for the task before giving out the kit.

4. When they have built their shelter ask everyone to walk around and look at each other's.

5. Discuss how difficult it was to build the shelter with their disabilities. What strategies did they use? What emotions did they experience and how did they manage them?

KS2/3

1. Share the story with the children. They are lost in the Arctic and need to build a shelter. If in groups of 4, 3 of them have snow blindness and so are not able to see. Their leader has frostbite on their hands so cannot touch anything. Together they have to build a model shelter from the kit provided.

2. Tell the children that they have 30 minutes to build their shelter.

3. Blindfold the child who is going to have snow blindness for the task before giving out the kit.

4. When they have built their shelter, ask everyone to walk around and look at each other's.

5. Discuss how difficult it was to build the shelter with their disabilities. What strategies did they use? What emotions did they experience and how did they manage them?

6. Share the Problem Solving Cycle with them and discuss.

7. How important do they think being adaptable is in the problem solving process – give it a rate out of 10?

RESOURCES

1. Elastic bands

2. Lolly pop sticks

3. 1m of string

4. Blue tack

5. Toothpicks

6. Card

7. Plastic bag

8. Scissors

9. 4 paperclips

10. 4 split pins

11. A rubber

12. Problem Solving Cycle

13. Blindfolds

IMPORTANT POINTS

Being flexible and adaptable are both important when problem solving.

Communication is vital when problem solving as part of a team.

LEARNING LINKS

Teamwork, problem solving, creativity, speaking and listening.

REFLECTION

Questions:

Positive comment from child:

Positive comment from adult:

LEARNING DIMENSIONS		SOCIAL & EMOTIONAL SKILLS	
Strategic awareness		Emotional literacy	
Learning relationships		Neuroscience	
Curiosity		Self-regulation	
Creativity		Self-development	
Meaning making			
Changing & learning			
Resilience			

Problem Solving

Defining the problem

Is there a problem?

What is the problem?

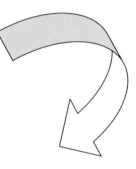

Evaluating progress

Did the plan work?

What needs to happen next?

Analysing the problem

Why is it happening?

Creating a plan

Following the plan

Exploring the options of what to do

Listing options and consequences

Problem solving 2

SESSION OBJECTIVES

To explore problem solving strategies.

To work within a group to solve a problem.

To understand the importance of collaboration when trying to solve problems.

SESSION OUTCOMES

✓ To create a story together as a class.

✓ To understand and be able to give examples of ways that they have collaborated with each other to solve a problem.

LESSON PLAN

➢ Ask the children to remember a time when their class baby had a story read to them. Did they enjoy it? Did they enjoy looking at the pictures and engaging with the story?

For those classrooms not able to undertake the Circles for Learning Project, video clips or photographs can be used to support the discussion around the topic and stimulate thoughts and ideas from the children and young people.

Task

KS1/KS2/KS3: To create a story as a group.

1. Ask the children to explain the meaning of the word collaboration.

2. Why is collaboration important in problem solving?

3. Can they give an example of a time when they collaborated with others to do something?

4. What are some of the problems that can arise when working/collaborating with others? What skills make someone good at working or collaborating with others?

5. How important do they think collaboration is when problem solving. Give it a mark out of 10.

6. Explain that as a class you are all going to collaborate together to make a story.

7. Sit the group or class in a circle and explain that the challenge is to create a group story.

8. Ask each child to choose a picture from the pictures face down in the middle of the circle. Or an object from a bag of objects that is passed around. Ask them to keep their pictures/ objects to themselves if possible.

9. Explain that you will start the story and then each person in the circle will add a short piece to the story so that everyone will have a part they will have added.

10. Sounds easy? The tricky bit is that the part they add has to incorporate the picture/object that they have chosen!!

11. Have fun.

RESOURCES

1. A variety of objects or pictures of objects

2. Whiteboard and pens

IMPORTANT POINTS

Working together in a collaborative way supports learning.

Collaboration includes supporting others as well as taking part.

LEARNING LINKS

Speaking and listening, collaboration, problem solving, creativity.

REFLECTION

Questions:

Positive comment from child:

Positive comment from adult:

LEARNING DIMENSIONS		SOCIAL & EMOTIONAL SKILLS	
Strategic awareness		Emotional literacy	
Learning relationships		Neuroscience	
Curiosity		Self-regulation	
Creativity		Self-development	
Meaning making			
Changing & learning			
Resilience			

Problem solving 3

SESSION OBJECTIVES

To explore problem solving strategies.

To work within a group to solve a problem.

To understand the importance of communication when trying to solve problems.

SESSION OUTCOMES

✓ To work as a team and copy and recreate a Lego® model.

✓ To understand the importance of communication when working on a problem as a team.

LESSON PLAN

➢ Ask the children to describe a time when their class baby copied something that someone had done.

➢ Discuss why copying is a good skill to have? Think of a time when they learnt something by copying someone else.

➢ How does it feel to be copied? Why? Now they are aware that coping is a vital skill in learning how do they think they will feel when they are copied in the future?

For those classrooms not able to undertake the Circles for Learning Project, video clips or photographs can be used to support the discussion around the topic and stimulate thoughts and ideas from the children and young people.

Task

KS1/KS2/KS3

1. Ask the children to remember which skills they have already looked at that support problem solving – what were they? Adaptability and collaboration – remind them of the mark they gave to each.

2. Explain that today's activity will be focused on communication. How important do they think communication is in problem solving – give it a mark out of 10.

3. Explain the task: One person from each team is the builder – give them one of the two bags of Lego needed for each team.

4. Ask the builder to go to the other end of the room and build something with the Lego – they have 15 minutes.

5. The rest of the team are given the second bag of Lego. Ask them to choose one person who is going to be the Project Manager.

6. Explain that the Project Manager is able to see what the Builder has created but the rest of the team is not able to see it. The Project Manager's job is to describe and direct the rest of the team so that they can build the same thing as their builder has created. The Project Manager is not allowed to touch the Lego bricks.

7. The children have 30 minutes to build.

8. Once they have finished, discuss the strategies and skills that were used that were positive. Discuss the things that happened that were not so positive.

9. How important do they think communication is now to problem solving? Ask them to give it a score out of 10 again.

RESOURCES

1. Packs of Lego, 1 for each group

2. Camera or other device to take photos

IMPORTANT POINTS

Working together needs a high level of communication if a problem is to be solved.

LEARNING LINKS

Speaking and listening, collaboration, problem solving, creativity.

REFLECTION

Questions:

Positive comment from child:

Positive comment from adult:

LEARNING DIMENSIONS		SOCIAL & EMOTIONAL SKILLS	
Strategic awareness		Emotional literacy	
Learning relationships		Neuroscience	
Curiosity		Self-regulation	
Creativity	▓	Self-development	
Meaning making			
Changing & learning	▓		
Resilience			

Problem solving: Solution focused

SESSION OBJECTIVES

To explore problem solving strategies.

To work within a group to solve a problem.

To understand the importance of exploring options when trying to solve problems.

SESSION OUTCOMES

✓ To be able to explore different solutions to a social problem, discuss the possible consequences and to decide which action to follow.

LESSON PLAN

For those classrooms not able to undertake the Circles for Learning Project, video clips or photographs can be used to support the discussion around the topic and stimulate thoughts and ideas from the children and young people.

Task

KS1/KS2/KS3: To discuss and then choose a solution to a social problem.

1. Remind the children of the Problem Solving Cycle.

2. Put the children in pairs or in small groups.

3. Explain that you are going to give them some social dilemmas/problems which you would like them to discuss together.

4. Ask them to think of a variety of solutions for each problem and then to write the consequence of each solution. When they have done this then as a group they are to

choose the best solution to the problem. If they are not able to agree then they need to show which solutions people like.

Ask them to think of a variety of solutions for each problem – the solution can be silly or sensible, funny or mad. Once they have come up with a variety of solutions, they need to cross off the ones which would mean someone might get hurt physically, emotionally or mentally. For the solutions left, they need to write the consequence for each one.

5. When they have completed their problems, gather together and share their problems – possible solutions and their consequences and then their choices.

6. Discuss the findings of each group.

7. Check that their final choice does not hurt or cause harm to anyone or anything.

RESOURCES

1. Problem solving options sheet

2. Social dilemmas/problems

IMPORTANT POINTS

By exploring different solutions and then understanding the consequences of each one helps the decision making process in problem solving.

LEARNING LINKS

Speaking and listening, collaboration, problem solving, creativity.

REFLECTION

Questions:

Positive comment from child:

Positive comment from adult:

LEARNING DIMENSIONS		SOCIAL & EMOTIONAL SKILLS	
Strategic awareness		Emotional literacy	
Learning relationships		Neuroscience	
Curiosity		Self-regulation	
Creativity		Self-development	
Meaning making			
Changing & learning			
Resilience			

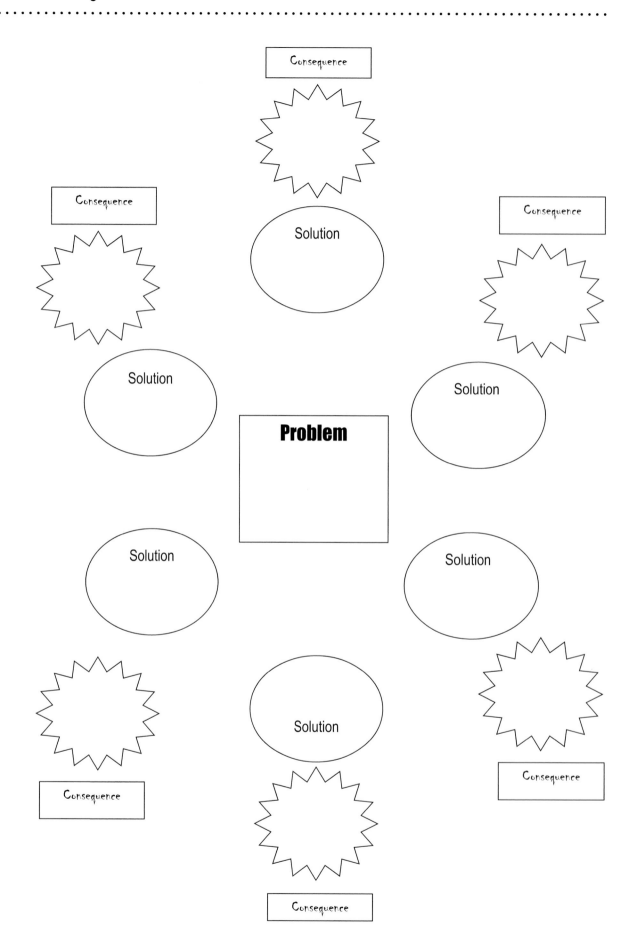

Consequence

Consequence

Consequence

Solution

Solution

Solution

Problem

Solution

Solution

Solution

Consequence

Consequence

Consequence

Problems for KS1	
You borrowed a toy car from your friend and now you can't find it. They have asked if they can have it back.	You are having a birthday party but your Mum has said you can only invite 4 of your friends. You have 6 friends in your class.
One of the children in your class has a new toy – you really like it but when you play with it, it breaks.	Some of the girls in your class are being unkind to a new girl; they won't let her play their game.
You were at your Dad's for the weekend and when you get to school you realise that you have left your friend's book at his house.	As you go past your classroom you see one of the children sitting in the corner in tears.
Your friend is really sad as their pet rabbit died at the weekend.	You go to a friend's birthday and have left their present in your Mum's car.
When you were playing with your friend you pulled their jumper in the game and it ripped.	You are doing some work in the class and your friend is not able to do it
You and your friend both want to run in the race but the teacher says only one person can enter.	You and your friend want to play it but the new child doesn't and your teacher has asked you to look after them today.

Problems for KS2	
Your get to school and realise that the project you were due to hand in today is at home on the kitchen table.	Your go to school and realise that you have forgotten your friend's birthday – you have nothing for them.
As you walk to school you see some of the kids in your class teasing the new child in the park and taking their bag.	You go to the local shops with some of your friends and when you come out two of them show you some sweets and tell you that they stole them.
You have a special match after school and you realise that the pair of shorts your friend lent you last week is not in your PE kit.	You have arranged to meet some friends in town and go to the cinema but your Mum has organised a family day out and you can't go.

You have been asked to look after a new child in school but they don't want to go to the field and play football at lunch time. You really want to play with your friends.	Some of the girls in your class are playing a game of It you ask to join in and they say no because you can't run fast enough.
You have used your Mum's special pen for writing and now you can't find it.	Your Dad asked you to wash the car and when you did you scratched it.

Problems for KS3

You get to school and realise that the project you were due to hand in today was at home on the kitchen table.	Your friends are all going to a party at the weekend but your parents won't let you go.
As you walk to school you see some of the kids in your class teasing the new child in the park and taking their bag.	You go to the local shops with some of your friends and when you come out two of them show you some sweets and tell you that they stole them.
One of the students from your class has asked you to do their homework or they will take your bag and throw it over the fence.	You have been put in detention for not doing your homework. If you go to detention you will miss your bus home. If you miss your bus your Mum will ground you.
You have been asked to look after a new child in school but they don't want to go to the field and play football at lunch time. You really want to play with your friends.	The girls in your class keep calling one of the other girls fat and stupid. She is getting very upset.
You are mucking around in the playground with a ball and you throw it at your friend. It hits him in the face and he collapses on the ground with blood pouring out of his mouth.	Your friend is being called racist names by some of the young people in another class; they are very upset by this and don't want to come to school.
Your friend thinks they are too fat and have stopped eating lunch at school. They tell you that when they eat at home they make themselves sick.	Your friend confides in you that they feel really down and fed up with things at home and that they are going to run away.

Chapter 4

Cognitive strategies

Memorisation

SESSION OBJECTIVES

To understand how the memory works and to explore a range of strategies to support memory and recall.

SESSION OUTCOMES

✓ To play Kim's Game.

✓ To explore and learn different strategies to support memory recall.

LESSON PLAN

➢ Ask the children to remember a game that they have watched their baby play that uses memory.

➢ Think of games or toys that use memory and recall to play.

For those classrooms not able to undertake the Circles for Learning Project, video clips or photographs can be used to support the discussion around the topic and stimulate thoughts and ideas from the children and young people.

Task

KS1: To play Kim's Game and I Went Camping.
KS2/KS3: To play Kim's Game and to explore a range of strategies to support memory recall.

KS1

1. Play Kim's Game with the children. Put 12 items on a tray and ask the children to remember what they are. Let them look at the items for 2 minutes then cover the tray with a cloth and ask the children to remember what was there.

2. Discuss the different ways they remembered the objects.

3. Ask the children to try and use the objects in a story as a way of remembering.

4.   Show the children a shopping list of 10 things (use the items in your shopping basket but don't show the children at this point). Explain to the children that at the end of the session you will ask them what was on the list.

5.   Discuss how many things they could remember and share the strategies they used.

6.   Share with the children the items in your shopping bag and then get them to visualise each item on a part of the body – demonstrate this!!!

7.   Put all the items away and see how many items can be remembered now. Lots! Explain that they don't have to have the items they could just imagine them on different parts of the body.

KS2/3

1.   Play Kim's Game with the children with about 12–15 items.

2.   Discuss the different strategies they used to remember the items.

3.   Share the memory sheet information with the children and try out some of the different ways to memorise things.

4.   Discuss which ones they found useful and why.

5.   Play a variety of memory games – The Vicar's Cat – going around the circle describing the vicar's cat alphabetically – first person thinks of an adjective beginning with 'a', second with 'b' and so on.

RESOURCES:

1.   A tray with 15 objects on

2.   A cloth

3.   A shopping basket with 10/15 objects in

4.   Memory sheet

IMPORTANT POINTS

There are different strategies that you can use to support your memory.

LEARNING LINKS

Skills for learning, revision, social skills, collaboration.

REFLECTION

Questions:

Positive comment from child:

Positive comment from adult:

LEARNING DIMENSIONS		SOCIAL & EMOTIONAL SKILLS	
Strategic awareness		Emotional literacy	
Learning relationships		Neuroscience	
Curiosity		Self-regulation	
Creativity		Self-development	
Meaning making			
Changing & learning			
Resilience			

WHAT IS MEMORY?

Do you have difficulties remembering facts, historical dates, people's names or how to spell words for a spelling test?

Your memory is a bit like a computer database. You can only find information/facts/dates or spellings that is in its database – The information needs to have been put in the data base first and then saved.

Your memory is really clever: it can store facts, sounds, tastes, smells, touch sensations, what you see, and even your feelings.

Using your memory is a bit like you storing files in different folders on your computer so that you can find them more easily when you need them. If you don't file things properly or you put them in the wrong folder or you can't remember your password, then you could be in trouble!

Your memory has three parts: Automatic, Short term and Long term.

Automatic memory – Is the memory that you don't even think about. It is the part of your brain that runs all of your body's systems – your heart for pumping blood around your body, your lungs which enable you to breath, digestion and keeping your body at the right temperature.

Short-term memory – is like the files that you are working on at the moment or the ones you use a lot.

Long-term memory – is like the stuff you save on your computer. You don't need to use it all the time but you know you can find it when you need it - well that is if you can remember where you put it of course!

Improving your memory

You can exercise your memory and label the information you want to save in such a way that you can find it when you need it. Your amazing brain does a whole heap of this without you even noticing when and what it is doing.

How many times have you been able to recognising a smell or a sound automatically? Not only this but sometimes when you hear or smell something another memory floats into your mind of where you heard or smelt that before. It could be the scent of camp fires that leads to the memory of one particular time in your life. It may be a song that reminds you of someone who sang it to you or the place where you heard it. Sometimes memories can flood into your mind without you having to think 'where and when did I hear or smell that?' So, if your mind can produce several memories all at once with just one trigger, then why can't you remember how to spell 'because' or 'helicopter', or which witch is which?

Well, the trick is to give your memory more than one way of remembering. You can do this by using more than one sense, (touch, sight, hearing, taste and smell) or by using visualisation

How to get your memory fit and ready for action
Here are 5 good techniques for remembering:

1. Visualisation

This is seeing something in your mind so that you will remember it - like when you take your PE kit out of your bag and put it on the floor under the coat rack. Think about the PE kit and how it is hiding under the coat rack and make a picture in your mind about something really silly like your football kit running and playing hide and seek. It will help you to remember where you left it when you are packing your schoolbag later.

2. Linking

This is like visualisation, but you link several things together.

Suppose you had to remember a list of things that your Mum wanted you to get from the shop. Maybe she wanted baked beans, bread, milk and cat food.

In your mind, 'link' them together in a funny way so that you can remember. How about little baked bean people chasing the cat trying to make it eat a bread sandwich and a glass of milk!! The sillier the picture, the easier it is to remember what you need.

3. Link to a place

This method was used by the Romans hundreds of years ago as a way to remember a list.

They would think of each object in a certain place and then imagine going to that place to pick it up.

For instance, if you needed to remember a list of things you needed to take on holiday then you could imagine one object in each of the rooms of your house. Toothpaste, toothbrush, hairbrush, swimming costume, phone charger, book, coat, wellingtons. Then imagine walking in your front door and walking around your house and picking them all up. Remember, the funnier the story the more likely you are to remember.

You walk in the front door and there is the toothpaste on the doormat, you then go into the hall and there is your toothbrush bouncing on the settee..........

4. Chunking

This method is where you break the information up into smaller chunks or pieces. The largest group of numbers that most people can remember is 4, so that is why credit card numbers or phone numbers are grouped in 3 or 4 numbered chunks. How do you remember your phone number?

5. Acrostics (say across-tiks)

Perhaps your teacher helped you to remember the order of the colours of a rainbow by teaching you a strange sentence like:

Richard Of York Gave Battle In Vain

Red, Orange, Yellow, Blue, Indigo, Violet

Use **mnemonics**

Small ants in danger – Said

Baby elephants can always understand small elephants – Because

Laugh and you get happy – Laugh

Mind Maps

SESSION OBJECTIVES

To be able to create a Mind Map® to support understanding of a topic and how different aspects link together.

SESSION OUTCOMES

✓ To be able to create a Mind Map showing information about a chosen topic/area.

✓ To be able to show how a topic can be divided up into different areas.

LESSON PLAN

➢ Ask the children to think about what is it like for a new parent – How do they know what to do? Where can they get information from? How do they know what to believe?

For those classrooms not able to undertake the Circles for Learning Project, video clips or photographs can be used to support the discussion around the topic and stimulate thoughts and ideas from the children and young people.

Task

KS1: To create a Mind Map as a class to show the different areas of a project that has been explored.

KS2: To create a Mind Map in small groups to show different areas of a topic already explored and how different pieces of information link together. The Mind Map will also include questions for each of the areas that the group would like to follow up.

KS3: To use Mind Maps to help take notes on a subject.

KS1

1. Ask the children to tell you as much as they can about a topic you have just worked on together. As they talk create a large Mind Map on a display board.

2. Ask the children to notice things about the Mind Map and share them – you use different colours for different aspects of the topic, You draw the map like a tree with different branches for different areas, you put illustrations to help you remember different pieces of information etc.

3. As you collect the information ask the children to start to guide you as to where it should be placed and in what colour.

4. Discuss the Mind Map – how they think it could be useful? How they might use it?

KS2/3

1. Remind the children about Mind Maps and how they work – give a quick demonstration.

2. Remind them that they can be really useful for revision and for note making on a topic.

3. Remind the children about the use of colours – different colours for different branches of information, drawings to support memory – their more interesting the more of a memory hook, questions that they may still need to find out etc.

4. Divide the class into pairs or small groups and explain that you want them to work together to create their own Mind Map on a topic.

5. Give out the reference books/information sheets to help them or ask them to find information themselves.

6. At the end of the work display the Mind Maps and discuss the different topics and how they found the work – how could they use Mind Maps in the future to help with note taking or revision?

RESOURCES

1. Paper

2. Pens

3. Pin board covered with paper – for a large Mind Map, KS1 markers

4. Reference books on each topic chosen/information sheets

5. *Mind Maps for Kids* by Tony Buzan

IMPORTANT POINTS

Mind Maps are useful for organising information that needs to be remembered.

Mind Maps can be helpful as a revision aide.

Mind Maps can be used as a form of note taking.

LEARNING LINKS

Revision, collaboration, memory, topic work, organisation, skills for learning.

REFLECTION

Questions:

Positive comment from child:

Positive comment from adult:

LEARNING DIMENSIONS		SOCIAL & EMOTIONAL SKILLS	
Strategic awareness	■	Emotional literacy	
Learning relationships		Neuroscience	
Curiosity		Self-regulation	
Creativity	■	Self-development	■
Meaning making			
Changing & learning	■		
Resilience			

Revision

SESSION OBJECTIVES

To explore different strategies that support revision.

SESSION OUTCOMES

✓ To be able to share and talk about a range of different strategies that can support revision.

LESSON PLAN

➢ Ask the children to think about being a parent – how do they know what to do? Where do they get information from? How do they remember what to do?

For those classrooms not able to undertake the Circles for Learning Project, video clips or photographs can be used to support the discussion around the topic and stimulate thoughts and ideas from the children and young people.

Task

KS2: To explore how they learn information best.
KS3: To explore a range of different strategies to prepare for a test/exam. Which strategies support them in learning and being able to recall information best?

KS2

1. Discuss how children learn information for a spelling test.

2. List the different strategies.

3. Explain that you are going to test out a range of different ways to learn spellings

4. Each child can try out 3 different ways.

5. Lay out on the tables the 10 different ways to learn your spellings with the words and the instructions.

6. Ask the children to walk around and read the different ways and then choose 3 ways that they would like to try out.

7. Try out the different ways.

8. Do a spelling test at the end and then discuss the results, which way the children preferred and why and how this new knowledge about the best way to learn would help them. Spelling tests can be spread over several weeks so that each of the different ways of learning spellings can be tested properly.

KS3

1. Discuss how the children revise – what methods do they use?

2. List the different methods:

   • Reading the information

   • Making a Mind Map of the information

   • Listening to a recording of the information

   • Writing revision cards

   • Bitesize revision or other web sites

   • Being tested

   • Old exam questions

3. Number the children 1 or 2.

4. Ask the children to write which is the method they use most often and then hold it up.

5. Ask all the 1's to choose a person who uses a method they would like to try and pair up.

6. Give out the information that you will be testing them on.

7. Working together ask the 2's to show the 1's how to revise in that way.

8. Change things over and ask the 2's to choose a person who uses a method they would like to try out.

9. Set the test for both the groups.

10. Discuss the results and what they experienced.

RESOURCES

1. A list of spellings/tables

2. 10 different ways to learn your spellings

3. A book/page of information on a given area or subject

4. A test on that subject

5. Access to a computer

6. Revision web site

7. Recording device

8. Camera

9. Learning Spellings information sheet

IMPORTANT POINTS

Being able to learn information and then being able to recall it for a test/exam can be done by using a variety of different strategies. Knowing which strategy works best for you is important.

LEARNING LINKS

Skills for learning, collaboration, revision, memorisation, exams, reducing stress.

REFLECTION

Questions:

Positive comment from child:

Positive comment from adult:

LEARNING DIMENSIONS		SOCIAL & EMOTIONAL SKILLS	
Strategic awareness		Emotional literacy	
Learning relationships		Neuroscience	
Curiosity		Self-regulation	
Creativity		Self-development	
Meaning making			
Changing & learning			
Resilience			

1. Flip It

Write the words on a piece of card.
Turn them all face down on the table.
Choose one card to flip.
When you have flipped it – read the word, spell out the letters in the word then flip it over so it is face down again and write the word on a piece of paper.
If you cannot do it or get the word wrong go through the process again.

2. Trace Copy Recall

Fold a piece of paper into three
On the first column write the word
On the second column copy the word
Fold over the paper so the words cannot be see and then in the third column write the word from memory.
If you cannot remember or get the word wrong go through the process again.

3. Look Cover Write

Look at the word – try to remember how it looks.
Cover the word up.
Write the word on a piece of paper.
Check the word is spelt correctly.
If you can't remember how to spell the word start the process again.
If you get the word incorrect follow the process again.

4. Rainbow Write

Write the word in each of the colours of the rainbow –red, orange, yellow, green, blue, indigo, violet.
When you have done this turn over the piece of paper and then write from memory the word using a different colour for each letter.

5. Word Scramble

Write the letters of the word on small pieces of paper.
Mix up the pieces.
Unscramble the word to make the correct word.
Check that you have made it correctly.
Write the word on your list without looking.

6. Word Stairs

Write the first letter of the word.
Underneath write the first two letters.
Underneath write the first three letters.
S
SP
SPE
SPEL
SPELL

7. 3 Bears – Big Medium and Little

Write the word as big as you can.
Write the word in a medium size.
Write the word as small as you can.

8. Flashlight Words

Drape a table with a cloth.
Attach the letter board to the table so it hangs down and you can see it.
Sitting in the dark shine your flashlight at each letter in the correct order to spell the word saying the letters as you go.

9. Feel It

Using sand in a tray copy the letters of the word into the sand saying the letters as you go.
Rub out the word and now write the letters with your eyes shut but saying the letters.
If you cannot do it or get it wrong, follow the process again.

10. Hopscotch Spelling

On A4 paper, write the letters that make up the first word.
Lay the letters on the floor in a hopscotch pattern.
Hop on the correct letters, saying them as you go to spell out the word.

a	b	c	d
e	f	g	h
i	j	k	l
m	n	o	p
q	r	s	t
u	v	w	x
y	z		

Bibliography

'**Baby first steps – Learning to walk music video',** https://www.youtube.com/watch?v=GOoquu Oq49I (accessed 29 December 2018).

Beard, R.M. (1969). *An Outline of Piaget's Developmental Psychology.* London: Routledge and Kegan Paul Ltd.

Becker, A. (2014). *The Journey.* London: Walker Books.

Buzan, T. (2003). *Mind Maps for Kids.* London: Thorsons.

Claxton, G. (2004). 'Learning is learnable (and we ought to teach it).' In J. Cassell (ed.) *Ten Years On* report. National Commission for Education, University of Brighton.

Claxton, G., Chambers, M., Powell, G. H., and Lucas, B. (2011). *The Learning Powered School: Pioneering 21st Century Education.* Bristol: TLO Limited.

Cook, J. (2012). *Teamwork Isn't My Thing and I Don't Like to Share.* Nebraska: Boys Town Press.

Crick, R. D., Broadfoot, P., & Claxton, G. (2004). 'Developing an effective lifelong learning inventory: the ELLI project', *Assessment in Education: Principles, Policy & Practice,* 11(3), 247–272.

Deacon, A. and Schwartz, V. (2015). *I am Henry Finch.* London: Walker Books.

De Lestrade, A. and Docampo, V. (2010). *Phileas's Fortune: A Story about Self-expression.* Washington, DC: Magination Press.

'**Dr Siegel's hand model of the brain',** https://www.youtube.com/watch?v=f-m2YcdMdFw (accessed 6 November 2018).

Education Endowment Foundation (2018). *Metacognition and Self-regulated Learning: A Guidance Report.* London: Education Endowment Foundation.

Fosnot, C. T., & Perry, R. S. (1996). 'Constructivism: A psychological theory of learning', *Constructivism: Theory, Perspectives, and Practice,* 2, 8–33.

Greder, A. (2008). *The Island.* Sydney: Allen and Unwin.

Habben, D. (2019). *Mr Sherman's Cloud.* Salem, MA: Page Street Kids.

Bibliography

Hamanaka, S. (1996). *Peace Crane.* New York: William Morrow.

Harvey, N. (2018). *Silly Limbic.* Naomi Harvey.

'Inspiring Heather Dorniden takes a fall but still wins the race', https://www.youtube.com/watch?v=xjejTQdK5OI (accessed 29 December 2018).

Kwan, C. (2015). 'How to give a presentation about a product', https://www.youtube.com/watch?v=U6H5j3FkIHA (accessed 29 December 2018).

Mack, J. (2012). *Good News Bad News.* San Francisco: Chronicle Books.

Malcom, D. (2015). *Meh.* Las Vegas: ThunderStone Books.

Montessori, M. (2004). *The Discovery of the Child.* New Delhi: Aakar Books.

Muth, J. J. (2002). *The Three Questions.* New York: Scholastic US.

NHS Fife (2011). 'Relax like a cat: Relaxation for children', http://www.moodcafe.co.uk/media/26930/Relaxleaflet.pdf (accessed 29 December 2018).

Peltzman, B. R. (1998). *Pioneers of Early Childhood Education: A Bio-bibliographical Guide.* Westport, CT: Greenwood Press.

Open Learning from the Open University (2015). 'Alexander Fleming and the Accidental Mould Juice – The Serendipity of Science (2/3)', https://www.youtube.com/watch?v=OZWjzcsTd5M (accessed 29 December 2018).

Popov, N. (1998). *Why?* New York: North South Books.

Pound, L. (2005). *How Children Learn: From Montessori to Vygotsky – Educational Theories and Approaches Made Easy.* London: Step Forward Publishing.

Reynolds, P. and Reynolds, P. (2014). *Going Places.* New York: Atheneum Books for Young Readers.

Rule the Room (2013). 'How to do a presentation – 5 steps to a killer opener', https://www.youtube.com/watch?v=dEDcc0aCjaA (accessed 29 December 2018).

Sniegoski, S. J. (1994). *Froebel and Early Childhood Education in America.* EDRS, https://files.eric.ed.gov/fulltext/ED385386.pdf (accessed 29 December 2018).

Spires, A. (2017). *The Most Magnificent Thing.* Toronto: Kids Can Press.

The Mindful Word (2012). 'Guided imagery scripts for kids: The big white house', https://www. themindfulword.org/2012/guided-imagery-scripts-children-anxiety-stress/ (accessed 29 December 2018).

'Toddler learning to stand and walk', https://www.youtube.com/watch?v=vO6EQgzqvWg (accessed 29 December 2018).

Waber, B. (2002). *Courage.* Boston: Houghton Mifflin.

Walton, K. J. (2013). *I Can't Do This.* K. J. Walton.

Wimmer, S. (2012). *The Word Collector.* Madrid: Cuento de Luz.

Yabuki, A. (2016). *Ishi.* New York: Powerhouse Books.

Yamada, K. (2014). *What Do You Do with an Idea?* London: Compendium Publishing.